# Individual and State
# in Ancient China

# Individual and State in Ancient China

## Essays on Four Chinese Philosophers

by Vitaly A. Rubin

Translated by Steven I Levine

Columbia University Press · New York · 1976

Acknowledgment is made to
The Kadoorie Family Fund for Chinese Studies—a project of
the Fund for Higher Education (in Israel)—
for assistance in publication of this volume


Library of Congress Cataloging in Publication Data

Rubin, Vitalii Aronovich.
  Individual and state in ancient China.

  Translation of Ideologiia i kul'tura drevnego
Kitaia.
  Bibliography: p.
  Includes index.
  1. Philosophy, Chinese.  I. Title.
B126.R813       181'.11      76–4516
ISBN 0–231–04064–4


Columbia University Press
New York  Guildford, Surrey

To the memory of my father and friend Aaron Ilich Rubin

# CONTENTS

# FOREWORD

In the ordinary course of things *Individual and State in Ancient China* would not have come into the hands of English readers but would have suffered the oblivion intended for it by the wardens of independent thought in the Soviet Union. To Steven Levine, however, there was something compelling in the underlying human problems to which the work addresses itself, as well as in the human situation of the author, that led him, though a student of modern Chinese politics rather than of ancient Chinese philosophy, to a personal involvement with the fate of Rubin as a scholar and a man and to the translating of this book.

One cannot claim for Rubin's work that it is the fruit of highly original research or the product of newly discovered materials. He has had no access to previously unknown texts. If anything, working in isolation and handicapped by restrictions on his movements, he has experienced extraordinary difficulty in keeping up even with other work in the field. Hence these essays make no claim to being exhaustive or definitive; instead their singular merit and appeal are to be found in the interpretive insights and unusual perspectives afforded by Rubin's personal experience in the twentieth century of problems already agitating classical Chinese thinkers in the sixth and fifth centuries B.C.

What strikes one immediately in Rubin's work is its freedom from ideological preconceptions and sterile typologies. That such an independent standpoint could emerge in an atmosphere heavy with dogmatic definitions and befogged by partisan polemics, takes us quite by surprise—less expectable even than Solzhenitsyn's volcanic eruption from the Gulag Archipelago.

Through all the doctrinaire stereotypes of good guys and bad guys in ancient China, and in the face of the modern anti-Confucian campaign, Rubin has come to his own appreciation of Confucius' unassuming greatness and capacity to inspire even a brutalized generation of men.

WM. THEODORE DE BARY

April 1976

# TRANSLATOR'S PREFACE

The lives of most scholars are of little interest to any but the inveterately curious. It may seem odd to insist, therefore, that it is important to know something about Vitaly A. Rubin's life in order to understand his book on ancient Chinese thought. But this is undoubtedly so. *Individual and State in Ancient China* is the product of a man whose experiences in life brought him to the study of ancient Chinese thought as part of an intense quest for answers to basic human questions. As he states in his Introduction, this quest proceeded from the assumption that "living in the second half of the twentieth century in the USSR, I could derive something of essential value for myself in Chinese writings of the second half of the first millenium B.C." The conviction that basic ethical problems can be approached in a manner transcending the boundaries of time and place is a well-established tradition in the study of political philosophy. Yet the perspective which any author brings to bear on the study of these problems cannot be divorced from his own particular circumstances. In Rubin's case, as Professor Wm. Theodore de Bary of Columbia University has aptly observed, "no one in the West without [his] experience of life in the Soviet Union, has been able to draw out of ancient Chinese Legalism and Confucianism the same significance Rubin does."

Many Western scholars first became acquainted with the name of Vitaly Rubin through the "Letters" column of the *New York Review of Books* (October 5,1972). "Is the scholar human?" he asked. His brief letter told a story all too familiar in many respects. A Senior Research Fellow in Chinese Studies at Moscow's Institute of Oriental Studies, Dr. Rubin, like so many Russian Jews, had, in February 1972, applied for an exit visa to emigrate

to Israel, which he considers his homeland. Rubin, a prolific
scholar in the field of ancient Chinese history and thought, was
pressured into resigning his position at the Institute. Subsequently, his works were withdrawn from circulation, citations
of his writings disappeared, and many of his professional colleagues shunned him. After months of anxious waiting, Rubin
was denied his visa, ostensibly on the grounds that he was "an
important specialist" whose services were needed in the USSR.
Dr. Rubin then turned to his foreign colleagues, appealing to
them in his brief letter for help in his time of need.

How does one respond to such an appeal? Western intellectuals are by now inured to receiving endless requests for ex-
pressions of sympathy and outrage on behalf of countless victims
of political repression throughout the world. To cope with the
demands for one's sympathy and time is practically an impossible task. Nevertheless Vitaly Rubin's own appeal elicited a spir-
ited response from within the international community of China
scholars. No doubt, the wayward heirs of Marx's internationalist
ethic viewed the resulting petitions, protest letters, and cables as
unwarranted intervention in the internal affairs of a sovereign state.
The present translation of *Individual and State in Ancient China*
is intended partly as a contribution to that legitimate "moral in-
terventionism" which is the only humane response to political
repression.

"Is the scholar human?" The shadow of an academic-po-
litical case can easily obscure the man who casts it. The broad con-
tours of Vitaly Rubin's life would seem unusual were they not
shared by hundreds of thousands of Soviet citizens of his generation, both Jewish and non-Jewish. That a man, extraordinary
perhaps only in his esoteric profession, becomes a public figure
and a symbol is a small sign of the times. Precisely because Rubin's life represents the fate of so many others, it is worth con-
sidering even apart from the light it sheds on his book.

From a brief autobiographical account written in 1973 as
well as from other sources, we learn that Vitaly Aronovich Rubin
was born in 1923 into a Russian Jewish family of intellectuals.
The life of his father symbolized the odyssey of a generation.

Educated in the orthodox tradition of his people, Aaron Rubin went on to study at the Law Faculty of St. Petersburg University, where he wrote a dissertation on Spinoza. But he had no interest in an academic career, and in any case the revolution of 1917 demanded a political stance which was alien to Aaron Rubin's nature. Consequently, his career was over even before it began. When the trials of the Mensheviks commenced in 1931, Vitaly Rubin's uncle Isaac, a prominent economist, was charged with possessing documents sent to him by Social-Democrats abroad (a serious offense in Stalin's Russia), and he was sentenced to prison and subsequent exile. Because of his brother's crime, Aaron Rubin lost his job and was compelled to eke out a living by doing miscellaneous translations from more than a dozen languages.

Family solidarity, which broke down in many Soviet families in the 1930s under the weight of severe political pressures, survived in the Rubin household, where the myth of Stalin was never viewed as anything but an abominable lie. The fate of Isaac Rubin was an intimate confirmation of this lie. Rearrested in 1937 after a brief spell of "freedom" (spent in Siberian exile), he disappeared into the fatal whirlwind of the labor camps and perished.

When war broke out in 1941, Vitaly Rubin, then a student at Moscow State University, volunteered for the army. He later wrote that, "As a Jew I felt my place was at the front." In October 1941, while Soviet armies were retreating from the German onslaught, Rubin's division was encircled and he was among the many taken captive. After three days, however, he escaped, rejoined the army, and fought in the bitterly contested battle of Kaluga.

In Stalin's Russia, escape from a POW camp was viewed not as a mark of heroism or loyalty, but as grounds for suspicion. With the war still raging and the entire population mobilized for national survival, special labor camps were established for former prisoners of war. Like Solzhenitsyn's fictional Ivan Denisovich, Vitaly Rubin was sentenced to hard labor in a camp coal mine. Even the most robust of men withered under the camp regimen.

Rubin, a slight frail man, toiled for eighteen months and con-
tracted spinal tuberculosis. Only then was he informed that his
name had been cleared some time earlier, and he was sent home
on a stretcher. Because of his infirmity he was confined to bed for
four years.

At the age of twenty-five, Rubin resumed his studies and
graduated from Moscow State University with a degree in Chinese history and language in 1951. This was a grim period in the
Soviet Union. The aging Stalin had unleashed new campaigns of
violence and repression which engulfed large numbers of Jewish
writers and intellectuals accused of cosmopolitanism, the Jewish
vice. In the China field, which Rubin now sought to enter, the
few who had survived the purges of the late 1930s were also subject to attack. (The famous Soviet adviser to Sun Yat-sen in the
1920s, Michael Borodin [born Gruesenberg], was sent to his
death in 1951.) Rubin, blocked from proceeding into graduate
studies, remained without regular work for almost two years. In
the period of "The Greatest Friendship," to borrow the title of
Mao Tse-tung's eulogy to Stalin, it was impossible for a young
Jewish sinologist to practice his profession in the USSR. Only
after Stalin died in 1953 did Rubin obtain a position on the staff
of the library of the Academy of Sciences in the field of Chinese
studies. This became his institutional home for the next fifteen
years.

During this period (in which he defended his dissertation), the range of Rubin's scholarly interests broadened to include Chinese archaeology, social institutions, and the political
philosophy of pre-Han China. His work increasingly focused
upon the theme of the relationship between the individual in society and the demands of the state. *Individual and State in Ancient China* (originally published in Moscow in 1970 as *Ideologiia
i kul'tura drevnego kitaia*[Ideology and Culture of Ancient China])
was the distillation of his thinking on this subject; it was presented in a nontechnical form that a general audience could comprehend.

Like the destiny of Solzhenitsyn and of his books *First
Circle* and *The Gulag Archipelago*, the fate of Vitaly Rubin and of

his book confirms that the current Soviet leadership dreads the power of the written word, even from the relatively obscure corner of ancient Chinese thought. Nor is this dread entirely a paranoid reaction. To be sure, not a few Soviet scholars seek to escape the confines of tacit or explicit canons of orthodoxy by retreating into the apparent safety of noncontroversial fields where the reigning orthodoxies are weak or nonexistent. There can be no doubt, however, that for Vitaly Rubin the study of Chinese thought did not represent a safe refuge, but rather a vantage point from which the present as well as the past could be scrutinized and judgement pronounced. In his own introduction Rubin describes the context in which *Individual and State* was written, and the official and unofficial reactions to its publication. Here we shall simply mention that detractors and admirers alike understood that the book served as an "allegory for the faceless intrusion of state power into his [Rubin's] own life and that of his fellows who value the pursuit of a civilized consciousness," as one perceptive critic expressed it.

Nevertheless, the minor furor surrounding the publication of *Individual and State* would have come to the attention of only a few foreign specialists if Rubin had not decided to emigrate to Israel in 1972. It is with this decision, born in the hope of a new life, that Vitaly Rubin's present ordeal began.

The related issues of Jewish emigration from the Soviet Union and the survival of Jewish identity within the USSR have occasioned much discussion in recent years. Here we need only note the obvious fact that the "case" of Vitaly Rubin is intimately connected with these issues. * Whatever the exact figures on would-be Jewish emigrants and their various motives, there can be little doubt that many Jews born and brought up in the Soviet Union no longer regard their birthplace as their own country. These questions, important as they are, form part of a still broader issue which, at the very least, is worth alluding to— namely the acquisition and assertion of alternate primary identities and loyalties by considerable numbers of Soviet citizens.

* Rubin himself, proudly Jewish in his identity, has addressed these questions in an essay entitled, "Moscow Testimony," *Present Tense*, Spring 1975, pp. 54–59.

Even without asking Andrei Amalrik's provocative question, *Will the Soviet Union Survive until 1984?*, one can easily understand the anxieties of the Russian leaders who rule over a multi-ethnic state. The tenacity with which nonassimilated Jews, dissident Baptists (*Initsiativniki*), nonconforming Russian Orthodox, nationalistic Ukrainians, Central Asians, and many others cling to their group identities in the face of massive official antagonism and outright repression is a political fact of no little significance. Moreover, to the extent that outsiders become interested in the fate of minorities within the USSR, their involvement becomes a complicating factor in the conduct of foreign policy as well. From the perspective of a Soviet decision-maker, the policies devised to cope with this problem must respond to domestic and foreign pressures without giving the appearance of weakness. They must help maintain maximum control, minimize the linkage of this with other foreign and domestic issues, and obstruct the further growth of "anti-Soviet" sentiments.

These general considerations suggest the question of what criteria Soviet decision-makers use in determining the fate of persons who seek to emigrate. Can some pattern be discerned in the vortex as to the method of disposing of individual human fates? What specifically accounts for the failure to issue Vitaly Rubin an exit visa when many other "important specialists" in fields more obviously relevant to state security have been allowed to leave? It is impossible for outsiders to say, but two things are clear. From the ordeal of men like Rubin, Soviet authorities want other prospective Jewish emigrants, especially those in the professions, to learn what the grave consequences of acting rashly are likely to be. (In this context, "rashness" means applying for an exit visa.) Secondly, to the "moral interventionists" who persist in assigning a definite ethical value to the fate of an individual, the message is clear—"Hands off! None of your business!" Of course the skilled Soviet dialecticians are by no means dogmatic. The changing calculus of advantage must account for numerous variables. As a top-ranking general in the Ministry of Internal Affairs told Mrs. Rubin in 1974, "Everything depends upon the international situation. For example, right now it is in-

convenient for us to release Rubin. When it will be convenient
we'll let him go." *

The response of Dr. Rubin's colleagues around the world
to his call for help deserves to be briefly chronicled. The files of
the KGB must be thick by now with the numerous letters, cables,
and petitions of protest addressed to Soviet authorities and aca-
demicians on the Rubin case. Only a few of the actions undertaken can be singled out here. In 1973, a petition in support of
Rubin was circulated internationally and over 1,300 signatures
were collected from individuals in the field of Asian studies. At
the XXIX International Congress of Orientalists meeting in Paris
in the summer of 1973, a protest resolution directed to the Soviet
authorities was passed deploring their failure to allow Rubin to
attend and present a paper. As a further response, it was decided
not to shift the next congress from Mexico City to Moscow, a
decision which evoked an unfortunate response from the head of
the Soviet delegation.

The present translation was undertaken in the spring of
1974 at the suggestion of Anne M. Birrell, and in October 1974 an
International Committee for Vitaly A. Rubin was organized by
her, Frank Joseph Shulman, and the translator with an office on
the Columbia University campus. It received broad support from
leading China scholars around the world. The Committee's
*Newsletter* is distributed through an international network.

The Hebrew University of Jerusalem, from which Professor Harold Z. Schiffrin has functioned as a dynamic conscience of
the profession, had offered Rubin a position in his field. At Columbia University, Professor Wm. Theodore de Bary was in-
strumental in extending Rubin an invitation to become a visiting
lecturer. Leading scholars too numerous to mention have spoken
out on behalf of Rubin's freedom and have taken action to assist
him in many different ways. In the face of the Soviet efforts to
isolate Rubin, messages of support and encouragement have
been transmitted through various channels, and books and sinological literature have been made available to him. Rubin's own

* International Committee for Vitaly A. Rubin, *Newsletter*, December, 1974, p. 3.

recent writings have found their way out with the aid of sympathetic travelers.

What is it like to live in limbo for years on end, at the mercy of hostile forces which treat you, at best, like a political pawn? For Vitaly Rubin, a man of great courage and steadfastness, the dulling edge of despair has been a frequent companion in the years since 1972. As he wrote in a message to foreign supporters in the spring of 1975:

> Each morning I wake up with the thought—three years have passed since I have been locked up here. It is impossible to wait. I have to do something, but I turn over in my mind every possible course of action and for the thousandth time, I come to the conclusion that every way ends up against a wall.
>
> I cannot help myself; there is nothing for me but to help others, as far as possible, to escape from this kingdom of violence and lies, to tell the truth and work in my own field. *

Nevertheless, the dominant impression carried away by foreign visitors who have met with Rubin is a sense of his vitality and optimism rather than this hopelessness. Somehow, throughout the long period of uncertainty, harassment, imprisonment, and illness, Dr. Rubin—sustained by his wife, Inessa, a teacher of German and Hebrew—has retained a joyfulness, warmth, and sense of humor that can only be called uplifting.

Not content to deny him an exit visa, Soviet authorities have carried out a campaign of periodic harassment. In May 1973, KGB agents searched Rubin's tiny apartment, confiscating manuscript and archival materials. In mid-February 1974, when Dr. Rubin and two fellow "refuseniks" conducted a two-week hunger strike, his telephone was cut off. It has never been reconnected. During President Nixon's visit to Moscow that July, Rubin and other political "undesirables" were rounded up and jailed for two weeks without any charges levied against them. Rubin's participation in protest demonstrations (e.g. against the slaughter of Israeli schoolchildren at Maalot in 1974) has also led to his arrest on a number of other occasions.

---

* International Committee for Vitaly A. Rubin, *Newsletter*, May 1975, p. 1.

The strain on a frail physique has taken its toll. On August 19, 1974, the very day he completed the Introduction to this book, Professor Rubin suffered a heart attack. A prolonged regimen of bed rest was prescribed. Nevertheless, in utter disregard for minimal forms of decency, the Moscow police, early in the morning of September 4, intruded into his apartment, roused Rubin from bed, and were about to take him off to face a charge of "parasitism" when he suffered a second heart seizure. No sooner was he on the road to recovery than the local procurator's office threatened to revive the charge of parasitism against him. Apparently, Rubin's continuing scholarly work is not considered to be socially useful labor in the USSR. As this preface is written, Vitaly Rubin's ordeal continues with no end in sight.

It is perhaps fitting to conclude these few pages on the note with which they began. Vitaly Rubin is not a didactic writer who bludgeons us with strained comparisons between ancient China and the present. But the things which he has "felt on his own hide," as the Russians say, enhance his understanding of the Chinese classics. His passionate, sometimes controversial, interpretations of the many-stranded Chinese tradition are rooted deeply in the convictions and values he is not ashamed to display.

This little book, then, is something more than another brief introduction to several of the major currents of thought in ancient China. Rubin's attempt to view Chinese thinkers from the perspective of the core concepts of authority, order, freedom, tradition, and culture gives his writing a multidimensionality it might otherwise lack. Through his inquiries into the intellectual controversies of ancient China, Rubin has successfully fused the specific concerns of the scholar with the broader commitment to truth which has long been the hallmark of the best of the Russian intellectual and Jewish scholarly traditions that he embodies so well.

STEVEN I LEVINE

New York City                                            April 1976

## PUBLISHER'S NOTE

Just as this book was about to go to press, it was announced that Vitaly Rubin had been granted permission to emigrate from the Soviet Union to Israel.

# PREFACE TO THE
# ENGLISH EDITION

When this book was first published in Moscow in 1970, I was extremely surprised. After all, I had written what I really believed in without the slightest regard for the circumstances that a Soviet author who publishes a book in the humanistic disciplines is bound to consider. If his work is not limited to marginal or highly specialized problems it must be fitted into and serve the general system of Soviet ideology. A work in philosophy must demonstrate the superiority of dialectical materialism and atheism over all forms of idealism and religious views. A work in history must confirm the correctness of the orthodox conception of the development of society from the primitive communist system through slaveholding, feudalism, and capitalism to socialism and communism. A work in literary or art criticism must demonstrate the superiority of realistic literature and art over all other forms of literature and art. In this context, the appearance of my book, which did not simply fail to conform to these requirements but directly contradicted them, was something in the nature of a miracle.

This miracle would not have occurred had there not begun a definite process of ideological erosion from the time of the 20th Congress of the CPSU. The iron cage had rusted through. Even in books that seemed to be entirely orthodox, there began to appear fresh thoughts; and in several fields works were published which in essence were not at all bound by the restrictions of official Soviet ideology. But by 1970 the process of tightening the ideological screws had already begun, and the possibility of expressing one's own thoughts in the field of the humanities was again approaching zero. To a certain degree it survived only in those fields where the material was new and unknown to the guardians of orthodoxy. Only because the Marxist classics had nothing to say about ancient Chinese philosophy (thank God they were ignorant of it!) could my book be published. The general reproach directed at me dozens of times at scholarly meetings and conferences—"an absence of party-mindedness and class approach"—covered a long list of my ideological transgressions. I did not point out the struggle in ancient Chinese philosophy between materialism and idealism (I did not mention those terms even once!). I did not explain which classes the ancient Chinese philosophers represented, thus rejecting the Marxist teachings about base and superstructure. Specifically, instead of unmasking Confucius as a reactionary, I outlined his moral philosophy sympathetically and valued highly the ideal of human personality he presented. Thus I intruded upon the ideological monopoly of the single correct and humane teaching—Marxism-Leninism. I analyzed the political theory of Shang Yang in detail, thus conjuring forth for the Soviet reader undesirable thoughts and associations—which such associations are usually not specified.

In creating the book I perceived my task as seeking to understand the subject matter, as well as the central idea, of each of the philosophers. This thought, which probably seems banal to the Western reader, will become clear only somewhat later, once the appraisals of the ancient Chinese thinkers in the Soviet literature are set forth—appraisals to which I implicitly objected.

The second premise of my research was the conviction that thoughts do not die. In other words, I proceeded from the assumption that living in the second half of the twentieth century in the USSR, I could derive for myself something of essential value in Chinese writing of five centuries B.C. I felt, moreover, that these ideas could be most relevant for me because, despite the differing circumstances in which we live, what unites us is more important. We face the same questions about the meaning and goals of human action, of good and evil, of the relationship to authority, and of the value of culture. Such an approach seems to me incomparably more fruitful and productive than attempting to deprive philosophical ideas of their transcendent meaning by emphasizing the dependence of a philosopher on the sociopolitical conditions of his time in a kind of historical reductionism. Some time after the appearance of my work, I noted with satisfaction that a large number of Western scholars share this approach. Thus Thomas Berry, in deploring the fact that contemporary man has lost his ties with tradition as represented by the ancient religions and is unable to accept the past in his world of contemporary values, writes: "What is called for now is not simply an extrinsic scientific identification of these traditions, but rather a new hermeneutics that would enable these traditions to continue; not as museum pieces of the past, but as vital cultural documents of the present." [1]

Confident that it is possible for humans to make contact across the broad expanses of world culture, I believe it is also possible to solve questions of interpretation in the field of intellectual history by addressing one's own interior experience. An awareness of my own place in history helps me orient myself in many theoretical controversies, and the study of ancient Chinese culture convinces me that man at that time confronted the same problems as he does now. If this is so, I have the right to resort to an experiment in thought through an analysis of my own path.

As an example let me cite one of the dogmas of Soviet Marxism: man's world view is defined by his class and social position. If someone attempted to analyze my views on this basis, he would probably come to the conclusion that they reflect the ideology of the Soviet freethinking intellectuals. He would try to explain my rejection of Soviet reality and Marxist ideology by the fact that as a Jew and a member of a family of Menshevik intellectuals, I never occupied any sort of important position in the Soviet academic hierarchy. But I know that my membership in this social group can be explained above all by my own choice. If I had decided to choose a different path and to win favor and political trust from the party leadership, then although I am a Jew and saddled by a bad social background, I almost certainly would have belonged to a different social group now; then my views would really have been different. But to explain them in terms of my social status would have meant to confuse cause and effect.

Viewing the ancient Chinese thinkers as living interlocutors, I addressed to them the questions that I felt were the most interesting and vital. These questions must also have engaged readers of my book, who noted at once its libertarian antitotalitarian thrust and bought up the entire printing within hours. From conversations with persons who had no relationship whatsoever with sinology—doctors, engineers, scholars, and so forth—I know the degree of interest with which my book was read. As a rule conversation began with an expression of incredulity about how it could have been published—the highest compliment in the USSR. Then the conversation usually switched to a discussion of the chapter on Shang Yang, whose misanthropic theories thoughtful Soviet citizens consider as a mirror of contemporary Soviet theory and practice. One must have lived in a totalitarian state where the only spiritual nourishment available is stale and lifeless Marxist dogma in order to really understand what freedom of the Word is. Even when it deals with ancient China it is taken as the bread of life.

It was entirely natural that a book which was warmly welcomed by intelligent readers did not please the Central Committee *apparatchiks*. Soon after the book's appearance, the publishing house which issued it received a severe dressing-down from the Central Committee for "relaxation of ideological vigilance." The reaction of the majority of official sinologists was just as hostile. They viewed the book as an open attack against both the ordinary methods of analyzing the views of the ancient Chinese philosophers as well as against the accepted interpretations of Soviet sinology. Inasmuch as the works of these sinologists are generally unavailable in Western languages, and since in my own work I had to take account of polemics although refraining from them, it seems appropriate to introduce a few brief extracts from their writings, which represent the ideational background of my book.

Soviet sinologists harshly condemn Confucius. F. S. Bykov writes that "on questions of natural philosophy Confucius accepted and developed the concepts of the preceding age concerning Heaven and/or the Will of Heaven as a consciously active higher force which defined the action and activity of men, and their social position." [2] M. L. Titarenko is even harsher, declaring that "bowing in all ways before the past and striving to restore ancient ceremonies and customs, Confucius formulated the principle of 'rectifying names,' i.e., bringing the position of the impoverished and bankrupt hereditary nobility into correspondence with its names and titles as a way to restore its past wealth and grandeur." [3] This same author writes, "Ascribing a great importance to learning and the education of men, Confucius at the same time considered that only the representatives of the aristocracy could possess wisdom, which they had as innate knowledge—the highest form of knowledge." [4] The texts of the Confucian classics are actually unavailable to the Soviet reader. The last translations of the *Lun yü* and the *Meng Tzu* issued in Russia date from before the revolution. [5]

In contrast to the Confucians, as early as the 1930s the Taoist philosophers were viewed in the USSR as materialists and dialecticians. They were the darlings of Soviet scholarship, and provided the opportunity to demonstrate that in ancient China, too, things had been as they were supposed to be: idealists in the guise of the Confucians met their rebuff from materialists in the person of the Taoists. In 1950 Yang Hsing-shun wrote that "the naive materialist teaching of Lao Tzu was deeply permeated by a spontaneous dialectical thought" and "the *tao* of Lao Tzu has nothing at all in common with any sort of spiritual principle whatsoever." [6] The essentials of Lao Tzu's social views resound like a hymn from this author's lips. "Burning hatred for the oppressors, sincere sympathy for the long-suffering people, and a deep faith in the eventual destruction of a socio-political order based on the oppression and plunder of the people—such are the basic features of Lao Tzu's socio-ethical teaching." [7] In the introduction to L. D. Pozdneeva's *Atheists, Materialists and Dialecticians of Ancient China*, which is a translation of *Chuang Tzu* and *Lieh Tzu*, it is said that in the atheism of the Taoists "their brilliant hypotheses about the unitary material principle of the universe and every creature are reflected." [8] As progressive thinkers should, members of the nonprivileged classes felt sympathy toward the poor.[9] All the classical works of ancient Taoism are now available in Russian translation.

Soviet sinologists accord a similar degree of sympathy to Mo Tzu. M. L. Titarenko writes that the school of Mo Tzu reflected the mental outlook of the free artisans of ancient China in their struggle against the hereditary aristocracy. Mo Tzu himself was "a prominent political thinker of ancient China. He put forth a series of profound hypotheses about the origin of the state, emphasized the role of labor in the life of society, opposed aggressive wars, and criticized the Confucian belief in the permanence and immutability of the privileges of the ruling aristocracy." [10] Mo Tzu has not yet been translated into Russian.

Until very recently, Legalism received a positive evaluation in Soviet literature. The sympathy of official Soviet sinology toward Legalism was first aroused by the fact that the Legalists were theoreticians of the centralized state and opponents of the Confucians. A. A. Petrov writes approvingly that "Han Fei Tzu denied the absolute importance and value of ancient tradition, the imitation of which under changing circumstances leads to social disorder." [11] F. S. Bykov discusses Han Fei and Legalism in a section called "The Teaching of Hsün Tzu and His Successors." He notes approvingly that Han Fei Tzu forthrightly criticized Confucius' followers for their summons to govern with the aid of ethical principles and ancient examples.[12] The most extreme devotee of the Legalists, E. P. Sinitsyn, declares that "Han Fei and his adherents came out against the Confucian rules and moral dogmas which fettered people and supported the privileges of the old aristocracy." [13] In Sinitsyn's words, Han Fei counterposed to Confucianism "a new morality which valued above all the interests of the state which played a progressive role at that time." [14]

Standing alone in the field of research concerning Legalism is L. S. Perelomov's The Book of the Ruler of Shang District—a translation and commentary on the Shang-chün shu prefaced by a wide-ranging introduction. Setting forth the theory of the classical roots of Shang Yang's views, and indicating their progressive character,[15] Perelomov at the same time writes that Shang Yang upheld aggressive policies and advised the ruler to encourage his officials to spy upon and denounce each other.[16] Nor is Perelomov ecstatic about the fact that "Shang Yang raised to the level of state policy the unification of thought and the universal stupefaction of the people." [17]

In these statements, significantly different from those cited before, new currents can be sensed. To a certain extent the possibility of their appearing in print was apparently facilitated by the fact that a year before Perelomov's book appeared, I published an article expressing thoughts similar to those which are basic to his book.[18] But it is worth going into more detail about this.

As the son of an original thinker who during the Soviet period was unable to have a single work of his printed and was constrained to support his family by making translations,[19] I learned very early that the occupation of a philosopher in the USSR was possible only within the confines of loyally searching for arguments to support the official dogma. Not the least reason for my choice of the history of ancient China as my specialty was that I hoped to be able to speak the truth while investigating various, discrete problems. The articles I published at the end of the 1950s and the beginning of the 1960s were devoted to studies of sources and the social history of ancient China.[20] But in the early 1960s I decided that it would make sense to propound my own point of view in the realm of intellectual history, which has always been the center of my interests. The general atmosphere of ideological thaw played a great role in this decision. In discussions a certain amount of freedom was allowed, although the debate was usually confined to scholarly seminars and rarely reached print. The worsening of Soviet–Chinese relations also tended to create a new situation in my field. Inasmuch as one of the points of ideological disagreement between the Soviet and the Chinese leadership was the evaluation of the 20th Congress of the CPSU and criticism of the "cult of personality"—i.e. Stalinist despotism—one could now attempt to treat the hitherto forbidden subject of despotism and the despotic ideology of Legalism in China. I saw that from ancient times the humanistic teaching of Confucianism was counterposed to Legalism and I viewed the struggle between these currents as the most interesting feature in the development of political thought in pre-Ch'in China. I understood, of course, that such an approach thoroughly contradicted the approved point of view on these matters.

In May 1964, I presented this thesis in a paper at the Department of Chinese History of the Institute of Oriental Languages at Moscow University. The discussion demonstrated that the time was not yet ripe for the presentation of such views. My colleagues unanimously condemned me for anti-historicism, for being oblivious to the class approach, and for slighting the successes of Soviet sinology. Not until three years later was it possible for me to publish an article in *Voprosy Istorii* outlining my views on Confucianism and Legalism. This was a real step forward. The very fact that one's article is published in one of the leading ideological journals put out by *Pravda* Publishing House is seen in the USSR as a kind of legitimation. Also it appears as an indication that a given point of view is acceptable within the framework of Soviet ideology. As a rule such publication paves the way for other works developing the same basic thesis. Moreover, the appearance in print of an unorthodox viewpoint presents other authors with a certain possibility of choice. My initial publication of a point of view new to Soviet sinology opened the way both for the appearance of my own subsequent works—in the first instance this book—and for works of those of my colleagues who were attempting to get away from the established scheme of things.

In conclusion I would like to mention something which is of interest in the context of the contemporary Chinese campaign against Confucius. As is well known, during the course of this campaign the Soviet "revisionists" have been accused of bowing down before Confucius and opposing the Legalist school.[21] The citations to the works of Soviet sinologists given above demonstrate the injustice of this accusation. In the first place, the dominant views of Soviet sinology are distinguishable from those in the contemporary Chinese press only in being less vulgar. In essence the position is identical.[22] Secondly, in none of the works of Soviet sinologists (with the exception of my own) has there been such a direct contrast between the Confucians and the Legalists. A reading of the aforementioned article convinced me that the thrust of the criticisms was aimed directly at my own views. This is evident in the comment from the Mass Criticism Group of Peking University and Tsinghua University which writes indignantly that, "the Soviet revisionist renegade clique . . . curse the first emperor of the Ch'in Dynasty Ch'in Shih-huang (259–210 B.C.) as 'the most ruthless tyrant in world history.' " [23] This citation is from one of my works, "Two Sources of Chinese Political Thought." [24] Thus in February 1974, the Chinese propagandists depicted as typical of Soviet sinology the views of a man who two years before had been purged from its ranks. It is difficult to tell whether the Mass Critics knew of this. Perhaps they did know but my views appeared more fitting to them as an object of scurrilous attack.

August 19, 1974                                        VITALY RUBIN

# CHAPTER ONE / TRADITION AND HUMAN PERSONALITY

## Confucius and Early Confucianism

### Historical conditions in the age of Confucius

The name of Confucius is known to every educated person. This is extremely significant and by no means accidental. A man who for thousands of years has been honored in one of the centers of civilization for the valuable truths he proclaimed could hardly be an unimportant figure. Nor could he be just a simple transmitter of what preceded him. Had he been, the people would logically have looked toward his predecessor and not to him.

The lives and views of men such as Confucius deserve to be studied not only for themselves, but also because every word of theirs which history has recorded is like a stone thrown into water—the circles created by it have widened across the generations and the ages.

Confucius initiated an unprecedented period in which philosophical thought flourished as it never has before or since— an age in which the foundations of Chinese culture were laid. His teaching was a point of departure for subsequent thinkers, some of whom continued and developed his views while others subjected them to a violent critique. But before characterizing his teachings, let us first review the essential historical background.

Confucius (551–479 B.C.) lived a little more than three centuries before the unification of China, at a time when China occupied only a very small part of its present area. It was divided into numerous city-states which still preserved to a certain degree the remnants of primitive democracy. According to traditional historiography this was during the reign of the Chou Dynasty (1122–249 B.C.) but in fact the Chou king who bore the title of Son of Heaven enjoyed authority but not power. He performed ritual functions like a holy person to whom Heaven had entrusted the rule of "all-under-Heaven," that is, the states of China which the ancient Chinese viewed as the center of civilization in general. These were called the Middle Kingdoms (*chung kuo*) because it was thought that they were surrounded by unclean tribes. This Chinese self-appellation has been preserved to the present day, the only difference being that now it must be understood as the Middle Kingdom (in the ancient Chinese language there was no plural form). The concept that all of China was a single all-under-Heaven ruled by a single person, the Son of Heaven, had the effect of making political fragmentation seem an anomaly, a falling away from the proper order of things, consequently temporary and transitional, representing a step toward a new unity. In ancient China no one conceived of the existence of states that were independent of the Son of Heaven and not subordinate to him. This exerted a definite influence on the political thinking of the Chinese.

However, the political reality was not all-under-Heaven but small city-states (*kuo*), which were populated mostly by peasants and, to a much lesser extent, by craftsmen and merchants. The number of households approached several thousand only in the largest cities. The upper stratum consisted of the nobility, which was related to the ruling dynasty and lived on income in kind from the villages. At this time slaves did not play an important role in the economy. They were used as servants in the palaces.

In the city-states [1] as a rule everyone knew everyone else, and to a significant degree the relations between the ruler and the subjects bore a personal character. This explains the deep-rooted, ancient Chinese concept of the state as a large family, reflected in the Chinese language where one of the terms for "state" is *kuo-chia* (state-family). The people in the city-states played an incomparably more active role than they did in the later empire. Although in ordinary times the ruler shared power only with the nobility, in perilous moments the armed people were gathered together, and the ruler dared not act without their approbation. In their speeches the most far-sighted representatives of the nobility constantly stressed that the fate of the rulers was in the hands of the people, advised that the people's interests be attended to, and warned against attempts to bind the people to the ruler's will by force of arms.[2]

As the Chinese historian Shang Yueh noted, such a political situation led to the conviction that the people were closely linked with supernatural forces, with Heaven and the spirits. Thus, in the Book of History (*Shu ching*), it is said that "the insight and watchfulness of Heaven are expressed through the insight and watchfulness of the people."[3] The chronicle *Tso Chuan* reports the words of a high official that, "the people are the master of the spirits."[4] It also cites the words of the chief musician of K'uang who, defending the right of the people to exile a cruel and unjust ruler, said:

> Heaven created the people, placed a ruler above them and charged him to be a pastor; he must not lose this quality. . . . Heaven's love for the people is great, is it possible Heaven would allow a single man to act arbitrarily towards them, give free rein to his whims and not take into account the nature of Heaven and Earth? Of course not![5]

A contemporary saying which later became a proverb also attests to this profound consciousness of the strength of the people, "The heart of the people is a wall, the voice of the people is metal."[6] The words of Confucius also bear witness to this: "Without the trust of the people, the state cannot survive."[7]

In addition to the city-states the organization of the *tsung-tsu* (clan) played an enormous role in ancient Chinese society of the sixth and fifth centuries B.C. As M. V. Kryukov has shown, this was a patrilineal organization, formed by a group of related families descended from a common ancestor. Within it there existed a hierarchical order, but the members were simultaneously bound together by common interests.[8] It was held that the *tsung-tsu* bore responsibility for the behavior of all its members. This explains the cases, reported in the sources, of whole families being liquidated because one of their members was implicated in a serious crime. The existence of a powerful organization bound by familial ties, together with the organic tie between the structure of the *tsung-tsu* and the system of social ranks then existing in ancient China, strengthened the concept of assumed identity of family and state.

## The life of Confucius. The Lun Yü.

Confucius, who was born in the state of Lu and spent almost his entire life there, was descended from a family of impoverished aristocrats. In his youth he endured many difficulties, and it may be that his early experiences and poverty were partially responsible for his life-long sympathy for the common people.

As the biographers of Confucius suggest, in his youth he tried to make a political career. But at that time the majority of official posts were handed down from father to son, and the really important posts from which affairs of state were decided were naturally the property of the scions of the upper aristocracy. A man of Confucius' background could have made his mark only if, through intrigues and flattery, he could win the favor of those who managed affairs of state. Confucius was definitely incapable of such behavior. Moreover, one gets the impression that later, whenever one of his pupils succeeded in arranging an important interview for him with the high and mighty, he always spoiled everything by openly expressing his opinion about the conduct of his interlocutor. One more opportunity was open—that of a military career. But Confucius felt a deep revulsion for killing, war, military drill, and the methods of military organization. Confucius always considered himself a representative of *wen* (the principle of morality and culture which arose in the eleventh century B.C.) which was opposed by *wu* (the principle of bellicosity and war).

Convinced that the path to a political career was closed to him, Confucius spent his time in scholarly research and teaching. Apparently, he considered himself a failure. In later times the activity of a scholar and teacher earned a certain degree of social prestige and sometimes even considerable renown, but in Confucius' day such renown was reserved only for the rulers and their closest associates. Of course, from the time the state appeared in China, especially from the time when regular chronicles were maintained, an acquaintance with historical materials was necessary for the daily conduct of both domestic policy and relations with other states. In just the same way it was necessary to know the ritual for conducting various ceremonies at the court of the sovereign. But this was done in an informal manner by officials whose basic duty was to participate in actual governing. The same was true of teaching and the training of successors for aging government officials.

Confucius was the first man in China to devote himself entirely to what his contemporaries viewed as secondary concerns. But most important, he was the first to concern himself with historical research and teaching in something other than an official capacity—and not in the course of discharging his official duties, but on his own initiative. The success of his activity demonstrates that the measure of a man is not determined by the place he occupies in an official hierarchy. One who ponders matters of justice, humanity, and culture will attract men who thirst to hear the living Word, and can play a role in the life of society incomparably greater than that of ministers and high dignitaries. This gradual discovery, achieved without conscious effort, was an unheard of innovation, a breakthrough to a new perspective from the anonymous collectivity of an archaic city-state. Living some 150 years after Confucius, his disciple Meng Tzu could already claim that a teacher was a much more respected figure than a ruler, and that not even the Son of Heaven, let alone a king, could command a teacher to appear before him.[9]

In all probability that current of thought which later became the Confucian school originated as the free association of friends who discussed questions of mutual interest. But Confucius' strength of mind and force of personality quickly led to his being recognized as the head of a school with his friends as pupils. The *Lun yü* mentions the names of twenty-two pupils, although Ssu-ma Ch'ien refers to seventy-seven. Even if these figures are inexact they give a rough idea of the size of his school. Confucius opened his school to anyone who came to him regardless of whether he belonged to the aristocracy or to the common people, to the rich or to the poor. He said that he recognized no distinctions among those who sought knowledge. At a time when family connection was the main mark of a man, this too was an innovation.

There exists in China a tradition that Confucius was an important dignitary in charge of judicial affairs in Lu. This tradition can be traced to a thoroughly respectable source—the biography of Confucius written by the great Chinese historian Ssu-ma Ch'ien (ca. 145–90 B.C.) whom we will refer to more than once below. Until quite recently the authority of Ssu-ma Ch'ien, supported and reinforced by a two-thousand-year-old tradition, seemed sufficient guarantee of the accuracy of this information. But critical investigations by modern scholars demonstrate that by no means should everything that Ssu-ma Ch'ien wrote be accepted unquestioningly. In particular, it has been suggested that because he lived under a centralized empire, Ssu-ma Ch'ien could not imagine the conditions that existed in the small independent city-states which had been destroyed over three centuries before his birth. Ssu-ma Ch'ien depicted the popular outbursts, which occurred in the streets and on the squares, as struggles among officials, which took place in the throne rooms and halls of the palaces.[10] Since he believed that emperors and their close associates created history in their palaces, it is not surprising that he transformed even Confucius into an official. For by then Confucius was seen as the founder of the state ideology. To Ssu-ma Ch'ien, the calling of a modest teacher seemed inappropriate for such a man. Relying on the legends which by that time had already enveloped the personality of Confucius, he attributed a high post to him and placed his biography among those of the kings and dukes.

The contemporary biographer of Confucius, H. G. Creel, has persuasively criticized this interpretation.[11] His central argument is that then only a person belonging to one of the noble families could hold a high post, and if Confucius had really held this position such a fact would have had to have been noted in the most reliable book concerning him—the *Analects* (*Lun yü*). Later, when legends about Confucius began to develop, it was alleged that as head of the judicial administration he ordered the death sentence for such crimes as "invention of unusual attire." We shall examine Confucius' political views below, but it is worth noting here that such a course of action entirely contradicts well-known sayings of Confucius, who was a principled opponent of cruel punishment.

However, Confucius apparently did hold some kind of official position. His pupils rose ever higher on the ladder of success, and this made it even more peculiar that their teacher was a person without official recognition. Chi K'ang-tzu, the ruler of Lu, conferred upon Confucius a title which was not very lofty but sufficiently honorable for the purpose. Apparently, he became one of the lower *ta-fu* (dignitaries). This is suggested by a passage which says that he spoke directly and unconstrainedly with other *ta-fu* but that he was more formal with superiors.[12] So far as we can judge, Confucius' position was one of honor, but one that gave him no opportunity to exert any real influence. Confucius found this difficult to bear. The *Lun yü* contains the following anecdote. One of Confucius' pupils was late for an appointment with him and explained that he had been detained by state affairs. Thereupon Confucius replied, "It must have been family affairs. If there had been government business, though I am not now in office, I should have been consulted about it." [13]

But soon he had to abandon this illusion and accept the fact that he would never succeed in achieving political influence in Lu. Meanwhile, he was approaching sixty, and if he wanted to act he could not put things off for long. So he decided to set off on his travels in order to find a ruler who would believe in his precepts and be willing to implement them. After wandering in various states of ancient China for about thirteen years, Confucius returned to Lu empty-handed. Several years after his return he died.

This unsuccessful journey stamped Confucius' life, which in general was rather pallid and poor in events, with the mark of suffering. In characterizing the meaning of Confucius' travels H. G. Creel has aptly stated:

> Assuredly his proper realm was that of ideas. . . . he was incapable of the compromises necessary to put them into practice. But it was extremely important that he should *try*. The difference is that which distinguishes an officer who says, "Follow me!" from one who says "Advance!" If Confucius had stayed in Lu enjoying a sinecure and strolling about with his pupils, he would have remained a preacher; by setting off on his hopeless quest he became a prophet. The picture of this venerable gentleman, in some respects still unsophisticated, setting off in his fifties to save the world by persuading the hard-bitten rulers of his day that they should not oppress their subjects, is in some ways ridiculous. But it is a magnificent kind of ridiculousness, found only in the great.[14]

Now let us look at the book that apparently is the sole reliable evidence concerning Confucius and his views and that we shall be relying on frequently hereafter. This is the *Lun yü*, a small treatise composed of the sayings of Confucius as well as conversations between him, his pupils, and his contemporaries.

The earliest Chinese bibliography, dating from the first century A.D., says that this book was compiled after Confucius' death by his pupils, on the basis of notes in their possession. But now most scholars agree that, with the exception of two chapters, the book—though actually based on these notes—was prepared 70 to 80 years after the death of Confucius, in the beginning of the 4th century B.C. The *Lun yü* is written in an extremely laconic style and consists of fragmentary notes dealing with the most varied themes, ranging from details of Confucius' daily life to an analysis of problems of philosophy, culture, politics, and morality. No system of thought is elaborated in the book. The chapters into which it is divided bear titles consisting of the first words of the first fragment. In rare instances several consecutive notes contain sayings on similar themes. The words of the teacher are interspersed with those of his pupils and almost always a variety of answers are given to the frequently repeated questions. The *Lun yü* records a constant effort of mind struggling with the solution of fundamental problems of human life and human relations. Confucius approaches these questions over and over again from different angles, each time suggesting a different aspect of their solution.

So that the reader may have a sense of the style of the book, we shall present several excerpts. Confucius noted: "The gentleman does not mind not being in office; all he minds about is whether he has qualities that entitle him to office. He does not mind failing to get recognition; he is too busy doing the things that entitle him to recognition." [15] The words of Confucius alternate with his pupils' recollections and thoughts about him. Thus, one of the notes says: "When the Master was in Ch'i, he heard the Shao, and for three months did not know the taste of flesh. 'I did not think,' he said, 'that music could have been made so excellent as this.' " [16] Another sums up an impression of his personality like this: "The Master's manner was affable yet firm, commanding but not harsh, polite but easy." [17]

There is an immense quantity of information about Confucius in the later Chinese sources, and until recent decades it was customary to construct the personality of the thinker on this foundation. But, as noted above, research carried out in the twentieth century has shown that these sources (the biography of Confucius in the *Historical Records* by Ssu-ma Ch'ien in the first instance) are unreliable and sometimes grossly distort his life and his views. We shall refer to them only in those cases where they allow us to elucidate facts whose reliability is established by the *Lun yü*.

## Tradition and culture

One of the distinguishing features of the *Lun yü* is Confucius' high evaluation of tradition as such. Because the stereotyped view of Confucianism as an essentially conservative ideology is largely based on this fact, it is necessary, in our view, to examine this question in a broader context.

The concept of tradition is most closely linked with the concept of culture, which may be interpreted in different and even contradictory ways. In their work devoted to this subject the American scholars Kroeber and Kluckhohn have analyzed several hundred definitions of culture.[18] The Polish sociologist Szczepanski has distinguished several basic meanings. First, a definition derived from the etymology of the concept, signifying in Latin the tilling of land. Second, a definition relating to the improvement and amelioration of human customs and conduct. Third, a definition by which culture is understood to be everything that does not develop by itself, but appears as a result of human labor, that which is created by purposive thought and action. Finally, an interpretation of culture which includes in the concept not all the creations of man, but only "higher things"—science, art, literature, and religion.[19] Szczepanski himself leans toward the third definition. He includes in this concept all the material and nonmaterial products of human activity, values, and modes of behavior, accepted in any given community and transmitted to other communities and to succeeding generations.[20] The definition which Yu. Lotman suggests in his work on the typology of culture largely coincides with such a concept: "the aggregate of nongenetical information which various collectivities of human society accumulate, preserve and transmit."[21]

Both definitions emphasize the prime importance of the fact that culture is transmitted from generation to generation. This is evidence of its indissoluble bond with tradition. Culture cannot exist without such transmission, such continuity. To conceive of a culture existing independent of tradition would be roughly equivalent to conceiving of a living organism in which the exchange of living matter had ceased. The whole complex of information, the content of the concept of "culture," lives in tradition. Culture is inconceivable without tradition, as tradition is inconceivable without culture. Thus, these terms do not indicate two separate phenomena but two aspects of the same phenomenon.

It is well-known that tribes and peoples at the primitive stage of development manifest a thoroughly remarkable respect for tradition. It is easy to understand the meaning of tradition in their lives—to put it simply, without cultural traditions, not a single one of these peoples would be able to survive. It is the very experience which the elders accumulate in struggling against the numerous enemies of primitive man and which they transmit in infinite detail to the younger generation that ensures the survival of the group. Since tradition is transmitted from the elder to the younger, in primitive tribes as a rule the old enjoy unquestioned authority.

But the ranks of people who respect tradition as such are not limited to primitive tribes. One may say that the urge toward innovation, the preference of the new to the old, is a comparatively recent feature which did not appear in history—particularly in the history of the people of Europe—until the beginning of modern times. Let us cite, for example, some material relating to ancient Rus'. Referring to ancient Russian literature, D. S. Likhachev remarks that on the basis of the psychology of those who read books in ancient Rus' it is impossible to assert that readers are always interested in everything new and contemporary. "In those times works survived for many centuries," writes Likhachev, "old works sometimes possessed greater interest than newly created works (they were interesting for their 'authoritativeness' as historical documents, or for their religious significance, etc.)." Objecting to those who see the traditional nature of old Russian literature as stemming from stagnation and insufficient creativity, Likhachev writes:

> The traditional nature of old Russian literature is a fact which was determined by the artistic system. . . . A striving for novelty, towards the renewal of artistic methods is a principle which developed entirely within modern literature. . . . Striving for the renovation of one's perception of the world is in no way an eternal property of literary creation.[22]

For Confucius tradition was embodied in the concept of *li*, which is translated into European languages as rites, etiquette, ritual, the rules of decorum, or as the proverbial "Chinese ceremonies." So that the reader may experience the meaning of this concept in Confucius' world outlook, it may be worthwhile to resort to an analogy with the rules of courtesy. Courtesy is absolutely essential for a cultured person, and even today careful observance of the rules of courtesy is looked upon as evidence of a person's high moral qualities. But this analogy, sufficient for a first approximation is, however, limited. *Li* is not only the rules of courtesy and decorous behavior, but also religious ritual, and the ritual of hunting, diplomacy, and governing. Lotman's remark that in medieval society every socially significant form of activity required its own ritual undoubtedly holds true for the archaic city-state of ancient China.[23] *Li*, therefore, includes not only the rules of courteous deportment; the form of ritual also symbolizes the religious views of a people, its cultural traditions, and its concepts of good and evil. The observance of *li* signified not only the fulfillment of certain definite rules; in Confucius' understanding, the acceptance of the values which were embodied in these rules was also involved.

Most of the time, Confucius uses *li* together with the word *yüeh*, which is usually translated as "music." This concept, however, is as little suited to precise translation into contemporary European languages as is *li*. In the first place, it means ritual dances performed in the courts of the ancient Chinese rulers to the accompaniment of musical instruments. In order to give some idea of how music was viewed in ancient China let us cite a dialogue between Confucius and one of his pupils, found in the "Treatise on Music."

> Once Confucius was sitting next to Pin Mou-chia and he struck up a conversation about music. He asked, "Why is it that in performing the song about King Wu the introduction and the overture accompanied by drumbeats is so prolonged?" "They signify King Wu's fear as to whether his army will support him," replied Pin Mou-chia. "Why do the sounds stretch out and moan like lengthy sighs?" asked Confucius. "In order to express King Wu's fear that his allies may not arrive in time," replied Pin Mou-chia. "Why do the dancers begin waving their arms and stamping their feet so early?" asked Confucius. "To show that the time has come to commence the battle," replied Pin Mou-chia.[24]

This dialogue (although apparently apocryphal) shows that each sound and gesture of "music" was thought to have meaning, symbolizing the thoughts and actions of historical heroes and helping one to feel the past as something inseparable from the present. The interpretation of musical works was by no means objective. Historically, it always was linked to ethics, to basic problems of human relations, and to society. This is beautifully expressed in the very same treatise, which says that having listened to such music, the gentleman will explain its contents, speak of antiquity, correct his own conduct and that of his family, and then will strive to establish justice and tranquility in all-under-Heaven.[25]

In Chinese tradition, ceremony (*li*) along with music (*yüeh*) form culture (*wen*). Both the derivation and the meaning of *wen* are worthy of note. In the Yin bone inscriptions of the 14th–12th centuries B.C. the character *wen* appeared as a pictogram of a man with a tattoo on his chest, and in early Chou written sources it is found with the meaning of "line, drawing, decoration." [26] Here there is still no premonition of the enormous role the principle of *wen* was subsequently to play in the world-view of the Chinese. It may seem strange that in a moment of mortal danger Confucius exclaimed, "If Heaven had really intended that *wen* should disappear, a latter-day mortal would never have been able to link himself to it as I have done." [27] Confucius traced this concept of *wen* to King Wen, the founder of the Chou dynasty. This identification of a quality with a particular man points to one of the pecularities of ancient Chinese thought which derives from the structure of the ancient Chinese language. In contrast to European languages, ancient Chinese is completely lacking in a category of time. While in European languages the very form of the verb indicates whether something took place in the past, is taking place in the present, or will take place in the future, in order to express this in ancient Chinese one needs to mention concrete names and events. In such a linguistic structure the fundamental difference between the past, the present, and the future vanishes. "A kind of temporal flatness appears, inhabited by various kinds of shapes and events which enable one to find one's bearings, but because of this flatness, time does not divide into two fundamentally opposing spheres—the past and the future." [28]

On the one hand this leads to the apparently permanent "presence" of figures from the past; on the other, to a deeply rooted habit of referring to historical precedents. If one adds to this the absence of grammatical particles, inflection, and suffixes, the result is that the possibility of forming abstract concepts is minimized. This explains the Chinese inclination to create abstract concepts through the aid of historical examples. In other words, a certain individual becomes, as a rule, the incarnation of a particular quality, and instead of saying "despot" one gives the name of a despot.

If this is so, it is impossible to determine the concrete meaning of the principle of *wen* without explaining the image of King Wen whose name, subsequently, in Ssu-ma Ch'ien's view, became a concept defining the entire government of the Chou dynasty.[29] Ssu-ma Ch'ien, who synthesized ancient Chinese tradition in his work, tells us that King Wen was distinguished by his exceptional moral qualities. "He was honest and humane. Respecting the aged and getting along well with children, he was respectful and modest in his relations with the wise."[30] Attracted by his virtues, the best people flocked to him from all over. This brought down upon him the wrath of the ruler of Yin, the state on which the Chou tribe was dependent. King Wen was imprisoned by the Yin ruler who released him only in return for precious gifts. Subsequently, King Wen succeeded in persuading the Yin ruler to abandon an especially odious form of torture by ceding him territory to the west of the Lo river.

This tells us nothing about culture as such, but in many ways it does emphasize King Wen's moral perfection. On what grounds can we include the meaning of "culture" in the concept of *wen?* To answer this question we must continue relating the story of the founding of the Chou dynasty. Although Ssu-ma Ch'ien says that King Wen accepted the "Mandate of Heaven" and thus ruled all-under-Heaven, in actuality the founder of the dynasty was King Wu, the son of King Wen. After his father's death, he raised an army and used it to destroy the Yin state. While the spectrum of meanings of the word *wen* is very broad, there is no doubt about the meaning of the name King Wu. It means the military king. And although tradition does not condemn the actions of this ruler, his image is sharply differentiated from that of his father. In the *Shu Ching* one can find a whole series of speeches which he made to his troops on the eve of battle, concluding with a threat of death for those who fought badly. After seizing the Yin capital, King Wu set off for the palace where the last emperor, Chou Hsin, and his wife had just hanged themselves; he cut their corpses into pieces.

This has not prevented the names of Kings Wen and Wu from being placed side by side in the ancient documents. Despite the fact that King Wen is more honored as the founder of the dynasty, the two are not counterposed in a moral sense.[31] However, the qualities embodied in these leaders gradually began to be recognized as profoundly distinctive and even opposed, and the principle of *wen*—combining peaceableness, morality, and culture—appeared as a contrast to bellicosity. This contrast is expressed in the words of Tzu Ch'an, a statesman and thinker of the second half of the sixth century B.C., who in a euphoric moment produced by military success in his native kingdom of Cheng said, "There can be no greater misfortune for a small state than military success without civil virtue."[32]

The term *wen* embraces a wide spectrum of meanings; however, after Confucius put forward the principle of *jen* (humanity) as his fundamental ethical concept, the concept of *wen* increasingly came to mean culture as such. One can already see this in the *Lun yü*, which cites Confucius' comments about how a young man should behave. Confucius says he must be respectful to his elders, serious, and sincere; he must carry out his promises exactly, show good feelings to everyone and seek the friendship of humane people. "If, when all this is done," Confucius adds, "he has any energy to spare, then let him study culture."[33] From that time on a popular theme in the political reflections of the Confucianist philosophers was the superiority of *wen* (understood as the way of peace, love of mankind, and culture) over the way of war.[34] Early Confucianism so deeply instilled an appreciation of the enormous role played by culture in the life of individual man and society that in the works of Tung Chung-shu, the greatest thinker of the second century B.C., *wen* figured as the underlying principle of the entire Chou period.[35]

## Two ideals of man

Respect for those who transmit tradition—the elders and, in the first instance, one's own parents—is always linked to respect for tradition itself. Confucius viewed filial piety (*hsiao*) as of primary importance, as the basis for all of the other human virtues. Among the family virtues he considered respect and love for one's elder brother (*ti*) to be second in importance. Lamenting that in his time children who simply fed their parents were considered to be exemplary, Confucius inquired, "But even dogs and horses are cared for to that extent. If there is no feeling of respect, wherein lies the difference?" [36] Confucius said that in accordance with the rules of *li* these feelings should be expressed during one's parents' lifetime through obedience and after their death by proper burial and the bringing of offerings to their tombs. [37]

It would be fruitless to search the *Lun yü* for a description of these rules. Arthur Waley was probably right in remarking that as long as they were carried out automatically there was no need to give them a fixed written form. [38] Therefore in order to gain some understanding of them, we must turn to the *Li chi* (Notes on Ritual). The section entitled *Nei Tze* (Domestic Rules) contains the most detailed prescription for the comportment of young people at home. After completing their morning toilet, the sons, accompanied by their wives, must appear before their parents.

> Standing before them, in a cheerful tone they modestly ask whether their clothing is sufficiently warm. If the parents are suffering from disease, illness or indigestion, the sons respectfully massage the painful part of their body. When the parents go out the sons and their wives escort them before and behind. They carry everything their parents need to wash up; the youngest holds the washbasin and the older the water-jar. . . . After the parents have washed their hands, the children give them a towel, and ask whether they need anything; if so they respectfully bring it. [39]

Equally detailed prescriptions are given for the rest of daily family life. Their leitmotif is obedience to parents, which should continue throughout life and not stop even when the children reach adulthood.

Such an appraisal of filial piety helped to ensure that this virtue came to enjoy exceptional social prestige in China. A contemporary scholar notes:

> Chinese society has always been thoroughly under the sway of the ethical concept of filial piety. In other words, it was built up on the basis of filial piety, which has penetrated into every corner of Chinese life and society, permeating all the activities of the Chinese people. . . . All traditional habits and customs of the people, collectively as well as individually, show the influence of the practice of this ethical principle. This observation may be verified through a careful survey of the family life, religious life, social life and political life of the Chinese people.[40]

Since the state was viewed as a large family, the virtue of obedience must also have found a place among the characteristics that define the relationship between the ruler and his subjects. And in fact, more than once the *Lun yü* expresses the thought that he who obeys the father in the family must obey the ruler within the state. Confucius speaks well of persons who are considered respectful sons in the clan to which they belong [41] and praises one of his elder contemporaries because, "In his private conduct he was courteous; in serving his master he was punctilious." [42] The idea that filial love and respect for elder brothers, who play a decisive role in the family, should serve as the basis of the subject's conduct is expressed by Confucius' pupil Yu Tzu:

> Those who in private life behave well towards their parents and elder brothers, in public life seldom show a disposition to resist the authority of their superiors. . . . It is upon the trunk that a gentleman works. When that is firmly set up the Way grows. And surely proper behavior towards parents and elder brothers is the trunk of Goodness.[43]

This call to submissiveness and obedience was one of the features of Confucianism which later, in the second century B.C., was to secure it the position of the official ideology. This theme, which in Confucius was still not stressed very strongly, subsequently became the leitmotif of imperial Confucianism. The philosophy of Hsün Tzu (ca. 298–238 B.C.) played a major role in this ideological evolution by stressing the necessity for a strict social hierarchy and affirming that man was evil by nature and could be rescued from his bad inclinations only by unquestioningly obeying his teachers. Etienne Balazs writes that the basic values of Confucianism, which subsequently ensured its position as a state ideology, were "respect, humility, docility, obedience, submission, and subordination to elders and betters." [44]

The idea that the state is nothing but a large family determined the views of Confucius on the most important questions of social order—in particular on the law. He believed that the law had no importance whatsoever for the improvement of society. It was important only that the state possess a good ruler who would instruct the people by his own example, and influence them with the help of virtue and the rules of decorum—li.[45] The chronicle *Tso Chuan* relates that in 513 B.C. the state of Chin cast tripods engraved with the code of punishments. Confucius condemned this, fearing that when the people became acquainted with the codes they would cease to respect the aristocracy, and that it would be difficult for the latter to retain their inherited positions.

According to the *Tso Chuan* Confucius said, "If there is no difference between the high and the low, how will it be possible to rule the state?" [46] H. G. Creel expresses doubt about the authenticity of this text, because no such argument is found in the *Lun yü;* Confucius never insists there that a necessary condition of government is that it distinguish between the high and the low.[47] It is quite possible that this argument was added by the compilers of the chronicle in the fourth century B.C.[48] However, an objection to the codification of the law is a natural corollary to the position of Confucius, who insisted that it is necessary and sufficient for good government that the ruler possess high moral qualities. From this time on, Chinese political thought contains two contrasting notions about the methods of rule—through the use of *li,* the rules of propriety which embody the traditional system of moral and cultural values, or through the use of *fa,* laws which signify strict and cruel regulation.

It is interesting to compare the Confucian contrast between law and ethical values handed down by tradition with the ancient Greek approach to this question. From the time of the Greco-Persian wars the Greeks recognized that the most important role in the polis was played by the laws and the constitution upon which the polis was founded. Law was seen not as a collection of commands and rules coming down from above, but as a charter which guaranteed the rights of citizens and defended them against oppression.[49] In the Greek classical age it was no longer even questioned whether law was needed. The real question was how justice could be maximized within the laws. Plato asserted that the only correct law was one that, like a good marksman, aimed constantly at true beauty and scorned everything lacking in virtue, be it wealth or anything of the sort.[50]

Confucius, by contrasting moral and cultural values with the law, exerted an enormous influence on the history of China. The question of the supremacy of law or the supremacy of tradition (the transmitter of the values of morality and culture), was posed at a time when the absorption of the city-states by the large kingdoms gave rise to the need to work out legislative and administrative norms. Statesmen and thinkers who understood the demands of the times accepted Confucius' dichotomy as beyond dispute and opted for law and, therefore, against culture and morality. Below we shall speak about the school of ancient Chinese thought (which in the European literature has been called the Legalists—*fa chia*). But here we should note that the cruelty which the proponents of this school praised and later practiced served to discredit the very idea of law in China.

The majority of scholars now view the call to submissiveness as the basic content of Confucius' message. Confucian texts demonstrate that this view is not without foundation. But still we are left somewhat bewildered by this. Indeed, how could it have happened that the propagator of such an impoverished doctrine, which offers so little satisfaction to man and does not correspond at all to the most important demands of individuality, could have received a place in the pantheon of mankind beside the greatest thinkers and the founders of world religions? How can one explain the survival of his teaching in China for two and a half millennia, its penetration into Korea, Japan, and Vietnam, and its resistance to such a powerful rival as Buddhism?

Can one really suppose that all of this was achieved simply through the propagation of obedience and submissiveness? If one turns again to the *Lun yü* to search for an answer to these questions, a striking fact is encountered: the message concerning obedience is balanced by one concerning disobedience. Replying to the question of how to serve the sovereign, Confucius says, "Never oppose him by subterfuge, but do so openly if need be." [51] This is not an isolated statement, but a principle found throughout the treatise. How can one explain this contradiction?

A study of the *Lun yü* reveals that Confucius had another ideal in addition to obedience. This ideal was embodied in the concept of the gentleman (*chün-tzu*). In order to understand Confucius' world view and penetrate the secret of his attractiveness, we need to explain the meaning of this concept. This is no less important than, let us say, for the student of medieval thought to understand medieval man's concept of the saint.

Confucius borrowed the term *chün-tzu* from the *Book of Songs* (*Shih Ching*) which Confucius not only knew thoroughly but, if one is to trust tradition, actually edited. In the *Book of Songs* the word *chün-tzu* signified the "son of the sovereign," or "aristocrat." (The literal meaning of the character *chün* is "sovereign," of *tzu*—"son.") Confucius changed the meaning of this word so that it no longer referred to birth but to the qualities of a person. The semantic evolution of this term is reminiscent of the evolution of the word "noble" in Russian. It originally indicated aristocratic birth, but in the contemporary language refers only to the moral character of a person. Placing the ideal of the gentleman at the center of his teaching, Confucius (although believing that he was creating nothing new but only transmitting what he had received from tradition) introduced an entirely new element into the ideological foundations of ancient Chinese life. In essence Confucius said that real nobility depended not on one's birth but on moral qualities and culture alone. Therefore, in principle, it was accessible to everyone. This not only meant the appearance of a new ideal in society, but a new type of bond in addition to the family bonds sanctified by tradition.

A conversation in the *Lun yü* among Confucius' pupils demonstrates that the people close to them looked upon the bonds linking these fellow disciples (all striving together for high ideals) as no less holy or unshakable than blood ties. One of them was lamenting that fate had given him no brothers. Another objected:

> Death and life are the decree of Heaven; wealth and rank depend upon the will of Heaven. If a *chün-tzu* attends to business and does not idle away his time, if he behaves with courtesy to others and observes the rules of ritual, then all within the Four Seas are his brothers.[52]

Numerous sayings of Confucius enable us to discover the ideal of personality which the word *chün-tzu* implies. Its most important characteristic is the quality of humanity—*jen*. Confucius says that the *chün-tzu* does not abandon his humanity either from haste or in times of danger. "The gentleman who once parts company with humanity does not fulfill that name." [53] Given a choice between what he prefers—his life or his moral principles—the *chün-tzu* will choose to die rather than reject that which gives meaning to his existence.[54] The *chün-tzu*'s aspiration toward high moral ideals is demonstrated not only in moments of mortal danger or in crisis situations, but is also embodied in his way of life, in his daily thoughts and actions. The *chün-tzu* is modest in his food and dress.[55] A man who is ashamed of coarse food and shabby clothing is not worth talking to, said Confucius.[56] The antithesis of the *chün-tzu* in this conception is the "small man" (*hsiao jen*) who is preoccupied with material well-being. "The *chün-tzu* thinks of justice, the small man thinks of gain." [57]

Confucius refers to justice (*i*) but this virtue (along with other qualities such as sincerity and loyalty) is in essence only one of the manifestations of the category of humanity which Confucius considers the decisive characteristic of man.[58] The very form of the character *jen* enables one to understand the meaning of this category. It consists of the character for "man" and the symbol for the number 2. In other words, the concept refers to the relationship between man and man. The words "humanity" and humaneness best convey the meaning. In the *Lun yü* the term *jen* is defined in various ways. The most suggestive and at the same time simplest explanation is when Confucius says that humanity means love of people.[59] In another place Confucius interprets it as a commandment, "Do not do to others what you would not like yourself." [60]

As has been noted, for Confucius the concepts of morality and culture are inseparable. Hence the demand that the *chün-tzu* possess culture as well as moral perfection. This is a specific feature of Confucianism which distinguishes it in particular from Christianity, where culture is entirely unnecessary for the saint. However, although Confucius and his pupils valued education and culture highly, they still gave first place to morality. The *Lun yü* cites the words of Confucius' pupil Tzu Hsia, who said that he considers even a man who has not formally studied educated if he helps his parents in a selfless spirit, is ready to give his life for his sovereign, and is faithful to his word in relation to his friends.[61] This apparently is a reference to a dispute among the pupils as to who may be considered a cultured man—he who knows a lot or he who behaves properly. The preference given to morality may be seen in another passage. Enumerating the duties of the pupil, Confucius says that at home he must behave respectfully to his parents and away from home to his elders, he must be favorably disposed toward all people, but seek friendship only with humane persons. If he still has any strength after discharging his obligations to his near ones, he must spend it on the study of culture.[62] The correlation between the spheres of morality and culture appears in a rather interesting fashion in a passage from the *Lun yü*, where Confucius gives the following answer to the question of what is a perfect man. The knowledge, talent, courage, and selflessness such a person possesses must be crowned by culture—i.e., understanding of music and the observance of ritual and the rules of propriety. But suddenly, as if realizing that his pupils, frightened by the impossibility of attaining this ideal, might lose interest in him, Confucius added:

> But perhaps today we need not ask all this of the perfect man. One who, when he sees a chance of gain, stops to think whether to pursue it would be right; when he sees that [his prince] is in danger, is ready to lay down his life; when the fulfillment of an old promise is exacted, stands by what he said long ago—him indeed I think we might call a "perfect man." [63]

But although culture, having yielded to the moral qualities, is absent from this "minimum-program" aimed at Confucius' contemporaries, the ideal of the *chün-tzu*, which Confucius explains in great detail, was nevertheless the ideal of a man who had achieved a harmonious combination of such qualities as morality, education, spontaneity, and refinement. This is expressed very well in Confucius' statement that the domination of nature over culture leads to coarseness, while the domination of culture over nature leads to the pedantry of officials who wrap themselves in bureaucratic red tape. True nobility arises only from the merging of nature and culture.

And so the *chün-tzu* exhibits a harmony of morality and education, ingenuousness and culture. Such a man possesses a broad tolerance, a profound understanding of life, and is revolted by any kind of fanaticism or extremism. Confucius called this tolerance the "middle way." He complained that because he could not find people who followed this way he was forced to address either the impetuous or the overly cautious.[64] Bearing in mind the need to preserve a proper measure in everything, Confucius said that to fall short was as bad as to exceed. The rules of propriety (*li*) help one to find the mean and to adhere to it. For the *chün-tzu* they play the role of a guideline which helps him to avoid extremes. "Courtesy not bounded by the prescriptions of ritual (*li*) becomes tiresome. Caution not bounded by the prescriptions of ritual becomes timidity, daring becomes turbulence, inflexibility becomes harshness." [65] A thorough knowledge of *li* thus becomes a necessity.

Hence the enormous importance which Confucius attached to love of learning. This is demonstrated by one of the most interesting passages of the *Lun yü* in which Confucius says to his pupil:

> Love of humanity without love of learning degenerates into silli-
> ness. Love of wisdom without love of learning degenerates into
> utter lack of principle. . . . Love of uprightness without love of
> learning degenerates into harshness. Love of courage without love
> of learning degenerates into turbulence.[66]

In another passage Confucius' favorite pupil, Yen Hui, described
the experiences of those whom Confucius initiated into the
sphere of higher spiritual and moral values:

> The more I strain my gaze up towards it, the higher it soars. The
> deeper I bore down into it, the harder it becomes. I see it in front;
> but suddenly it is behind. Step by step the Master skilfully lures
> one on. He has broadened me with culture, restrained me with
> ritual. Even if I wanted to stop I could not. Just when I feel that I
> have exhausted every resource, something seems to rise up,
> standing out sharp and clear. Yet though I long to pursue it, I can
> find no way of getting to it at all.[67]

The ideal of the *chün-tzu* is thus a conception of a person
who harmoniously combines morality and culture. One may note
the similarity between this concept and the ideal of kalokagathia,
which was developed in classical Greek philosophy; both are
concerned with the harmonious combination of disparate qualities. The difference between them, however, lies first of all in the
fact that kalokagathia (in Plato's definition of it) consisted of the
harmony of the internal and the external, of the soul and the
body; [68] such an approach is absolutely foreign to Confucius,
who assigned no importance to beauty or man's physical qualities.[69] Secondly, in both Plato and Aristotle,[70] kalokagathia is
linked with happiness; the ideal of the *chün-tzu* in Confucius is
of a much more stern, stoical character. Happiness plays no dis-
cernible role in it at all, and the obligation to fulfill one's duty, as
well as a readiness to sacrifice oneself for it, are constantly
stressed.

It is interesting to compare Confucius' notion of the "middle path" with the concept of the mean as a norm of human activity in the ethical writings of Aristotle. In the *Eudemian Ethics*
Aristotle compares the mean with a norm from which the physician determines the quantity of a medicine. "It will not work if

there is too much or too little." [71] In the *Nichomachean Ethics* the category of the mean acquires a universal significance in relation to all virtues. Thus Aristotle notes that when investigating justice one must explain what type of mean it is and between which extremes it falls. [72]

The idea of man as a harmonious and fully developed person is usually associated with Renaissance humanism. But there can be no doubt that the concept of kalokagathia, and the idea of the *chün-tzu* both demonstrate that the importance of harmony in personality formation was understood long before the Renaissance. This was noted by N. I. Konrad who wrote:

> It seems to me that it is a serious mistake to identify humanism with the Renaissance. It is beyond dispute that the Renaissance was closely connected with a movement which we may call humanistic, but this does not mean that humanism appeared on the earth only in the Renaissance period. . . . Humanism existed in both antiquity and the middle ages. [73]

The concept of the harmoniously developed personality (together with the enormous importance which Confucian ethics gave to the concept of humanity) is the most serious argument in favor of the thesis that the humanist tradition of ancient Chinese philosophy was formed within the framework of early Confucianism. In Confucius' remarkable words, "A *chün-tzu* is not an implement." [74] This shows that he viewed the development of the human personality not as a means but as an end of society.

This thesis requires substantiation from another side. Many scholars assert that Confucius was essentially a religious thinker. Thus Leon Vandermeersch writes: "A personal divinity can be discerned in Confucius' *tao*, even though it has become anonymous." [75] This opinion is supported by F. S. Bykov who noted that, "Confucius' concepts are basically founded on a belief in 'Heaven' and 'the spirits.' " [76] To what degree is this view correct?

An examination of the *Lun yü* reveals that Confucius was by no means an atheist. He interpreted Heaven (*t'ien*) as a divinity which to some extent directed earthly affairs. Confucius expressed this most clearly during a moment of mortal danger when, surrounded by hostile inhabitants of the state of K'uang, he exclaimed:

> When King Wen perished, did that mean that culture (*wen*) ceased to exist? If Heaven had really intended that such culture as his should disappear, a latter-day mortal would never have been able to link himself to it as I have done. And if Heaven does not intend to destroy such culture, what have I to fear from the people of K'uang? [77]

But while Confucius turns to Heaven as his only hope when on the brink of disaster, when conversing with his pupils and his friends in normal circumstances he refers neither to Heaven nor to the spirits. He does not promise other-worldly recompense for the virtuous, nor does he frighten the inhumane and the evil with torments after death. When his interlocutor tries to shift the conversation to these subjects, asking how should one serve the spirits and what does Confucius think of death, he replies: "Till you have learned to serve men, how can you serve ghosts? . . . Till you know about the living, how are you to know about the dead?" [78]

Confucius' teaching was directed at improving man's everyday life and, although he approved of the observance of religious (as of other) ritual, one gets the impression that for him, this was from one perspective a symbol of respectability, and from another a means of participating in tradition.

Sometimes the existing literature ignores the ideal of the *chün-tzu,* and characterizes Confucianism entirely on the basis of the ideal of the obedient subject. From this premise Confucianism is defined as a conservative ideology of feudal aristocracy, bureaucracy, or despotism. [79] But on the basis of the ideal of the *chün-tzu* we are compelled to considerably modify such appraisals. As a harmonious and self-sufficient person, the *chün-tzu* must not carry out the ruler's every command. On the contrary, he must resist when he deems the ruler's conduct immoral. If the remonstrances of the *chün-tzu* are ineffective and unscrupulousness and profit-hunting are reigning in the state then the *chün-tzu* must refuse to serve, [80] because honor and wealth dishonorably gained are not for him. It is shameful to think of enrichment in a state constructed on injustice.[81]

Confucius' negative attitude toward despotism can be seen in the words he addresses to the ruler of Lu, Duke Ting. In response to the ruler's question whether there is a saying which can cause the state to flourish Confucius says:

> No phrase could ever be like that. But here is one that comes near it. There is a saying among men, "It is hard to be a prince and not easy to be a minister." A ruler who really understood that it was "hard to be a prince" would have come fairly near to saving his country by a single phrase.
>
> Duke Ting said, "Is there any one phrase that could ruin a country?" Master K'ung said, "No phrase could ever be like that. But here is one that comes near to it. 'There is a saying among men: "What pleasure is there in being a prince, unless one can say whatever one chooses, and no one dares to disagree?" ' . . . If what he says is bad, will it not come very near to his ruining his country by a single phrase?" [82]

Confucius particularly stressed the *chün-tzu*'s nonconformism by asserting that the *chün-tzu* aims at harmony, not uniformity. Cheng Hsüan, a Chinese commentator of the second century A.D., in explaining this passage wrote, "A *chün-tzu*'s heart is in harmony with others, but his views are distinguished from theirs." This theme of autonomy, of the independence of the worthy and learned man, was continued in a number of later Confucian works. One of these, a small treatise entitled "The Conduct of a Confucian," is part of the *Li chi*. It waxes enthusiastic about the self-sufficiency of the gentleman—saying, for example, that the Confucian does not deem gold and jasper precious, but faithfulness and justice alone. If one should try to tempt him with riches and corrupt him with pleasures, despite everything set out before him, he would still not turn away even an inch from justice. "Even when power is in the hands of a tyrant he will not change his position."

That Confucius demanded firmness and courage of the *chün-tzu* is unexpectedly confirmed by the anti-Confucian treatise—the Taoist *Chuang Tzu*. It cites a conversation between

Confucius and his favorite pupil, Yen Hui. Telling Confucius that he wishes to set out for Wei to help the people who are suffering under the rule of a despot, Yen Hui says: "I have heard you say, Master, 'Leave the state that is well-ordered and go to the state in chaos! At the doctor's gate there are many sick men.' " [83] Confucius dissuades Yen Hui, saying first that such an undertaking is dangerous and second that one should not help the people, but strive to become a real sage able to discard all human cares, achieve enlightenment without knowledge, and fly over the earth without wings.[84] It need hardly be said that the Confucius of *Chuang Tzu* has nothing in common with the historical Confucius. The polemical device of putting one's own views into the mouths of the proponents of a rival doctrine is a well-known device in the history of social thought. In just the same way the Taoists later proclaimed Buddha to be a follower of Lao Tzu and the Christians said that Plato and the Stoics were pupils of Moses.[85] But there is something more interesting here. Although Yen Hui's words, which actually express the early Confucian approach to social problems, are cited in *Chuang Tzu* only to be refuted, in fact the ancient Chinese Don Quixote attracts the contemporary reader much more than does the superman indifferent to human sufferings.

## Confucianism in Chinese history

Confucius died 350 years before Confucianism became the state ideology. At the end of the third century B.C., when China was unified for the first time by the emperor Ch'in Shih-huang, the followers of Confucius were subjected to the cruelest persecution. Following the precepts of Shang Yang, who considered the bearers of culture—the educated and the intelligent—as a subversive element, Ch'in Shih-huang banned the study of ancient literature and philosophy, and ordered the burning of all books in the hands of private persons (with the exception of technical works on agriculture, medicine, and fortune telling). These measures, which were aimed at the complete liquidation of humanist culture, were accompanied by the execution of hundreds of prominent members of the intelligentsia. But the attempt at building an empire on a monolithic foundation of universal stupefaction ended in failure. Only a few years after the death of Ch'in Shih-huang his "thousand-year kingdom" collapsed under the blows of an uprising which swept the country.

The emperors of the following dynasty—the Han (206 B.C.–220 A.D.)—learned from the mistakes of their predecessors, and decided to reach an agreement with Confucianism rather than fight it. The Emperor Wu Ti (140–87 B.C.) proclaimed Confucianism as the state ideology, and this it remained until 1911. But Confucianism as the ruling dogma of the Chinese empire was different in essence from the actual teaching of Confucius. To the ethical positions of Confucianism were added cosmological speculations derived from Taoism and several other naturalist teachings. This entire mixture, moreover, was decked out in the trappings of religion. While religion did not play an important role in early Confucian thought, later in its development Heaven began to figure as a divinity, possessing moral consciousness and attentively following everything which happened on earth.

The emperor in particular, the Son of Heaven who was the center of the cosmological trinity of Heaven, Earth, and Man, was surrounded by a religious halo. He linked the trinity together, and as minister of Heaven's will he ensured by his just administration the strict succession of natural phenomena. While Confucius and Meng Tzu viewed the people as the most important element in the state, in imperial Confucianism (the name which this ideology has received) the ruler is seen as the center of the state. The ideal of the *chün-tzu* was also transformed. The dominant school changed him from a wandering knight of humanity into a model official whose chief characteristic was his blind and absolute obedience to the commands of his ruler.

Thus what has been termed the "triumph of Confucianism" might more correctly be called a Pyrrhic victory. But to confine ourselves to such a judgement would be to ignore that aspect of Confucianism which has played such an enormous role in ensuring the stability of the Chinese empire. This refers to the Confucian thesis that those who participate in government must be educated people. The proclamation of Confucianism as the state ideology was accompanied, reliable sources tell us, by the broad development of education and the establishment of a system of examinations that everyone who wished to hold an official post of any importance was required to pass. Of course, one cannot forget the privileges of the offspring of noble families which (especially at first) facilitated their entry into the ranks of the bureaucracy. Nor that the study of Confucian classics required a lot of money which the common man could not ordinarily afford. Still, the indisputable fact remains that as early as the second century A.D., Chinese officials were more often recruited on the basis of their general abilities than of their birth. This ensured a high level of competence in the ruling elite of antiquity and the middle ages. Until recently one could defend the position that the examinations were a fiction, designed to conceal the actual rule of a hereditary group of feudalists. But recent investigations by the American scholars Robert M. Marsh and Ho Ping-ti demonstrate that the examinations definitely created possibilities of mobility for talented persons from the lower classes.[86] Chinese literature also bears witness to this. One of its favorite subjects is the rapid rise of a poor but talented young man who has passed the examinations.

The establishment of a system of examinations for recruiting talented people into the ranks of officialdom had most important consequences for the fate of the Chinese state system and culture. The system promoted the cultural unification and integration of the country, because everyone who wished to participate in government had to pass through the same course of instruction. This very uniformity became a source of intellectual stagnation. But there is something else. Because the system provided a way for able people to advance, they became reliable supporters of the existing order. This made for a significant contrast between the situation in China and that in Europe. In the former, social protest directed against the existing order from within the educated strata was relatively rare. In the latter an important force which drove the best minds toward criticism of the existing order was the preservation of aristocratic privileges right up through the eighteenth and nineteenth centuries. However, the Chinese system of advancement for able people helped to secure support for the existing order even from a certain portion of the exploited lower classes, who viewed the system as basically just and saw its imperfections as caused by the abuses of individual officials.

The history of Confucianism is extremely complex and as yet poorly studied. Here we have touched only on that aspect which leads to the state ideology of the Chinese empire. However, one should not forget that imperial Confucianism, while connected by a definite progression with some of the views of early Confucianism, at the same time also sharply opposed other aspects of it. Some recent works [87] have suggested that Legalism, a teaching hostile to early Confucianism, played a significant role in the formation of the official ideology.

But a very different approach to the history of Confucianism is possible. In the ideas of early Confucianism, scholars have uncovered the wellsprings of the Chinese humanist tradition, which was continued in a number of medieval and contemporary thinkers. This, however, is a separate story.

# CHAPTER TWO / "STATE MACHINE FOR THE GENERAL WELFARE"

## Mo Tzu and Mohism

### The thinker: his personality, his times, and his books

Not much is known about Mo Tzu. In the *Historical Records,* Ssu-Ma Ch'ien devoted an extensive biography to Confucius, but there are only twenty-four Chinese characters in this work describing Mo Tzu. "Mo Ti was apparently a high official in the state of Sung. He was skilled in defensive strategy and stood for economy of expenditures. Some say that he was a contemporary of Confucius; others, that he lived later." [1] Subsequently, Chinese scholars established that his approximate dates were 479–381 B.C.; therefore he was not a contemporary of Confucius. In one of the treatises from the second century B.C., it is said that Mo Tzu was educated at a school run by Confucius' pupils. He apparently wandered through China like Confucius, trying to convince rulers of the existing states to foreswear aggressive policies and turn toward "universal love." Thus, one text informs us that after an exhausting ten-day journey he arrived at the court of the ruler of Ch'u who, he had learned, intended to attack the state of Sung, and persuaded the ruler to abandon his plan.

The sources tell us that Mo Tzu was the leader of an iron-disciplined, tightly knit sect of like-minded persons, one of whose aims was to aid states exposed to attack. In order to stay up to the mark, his followers practiced the martial arts and studied military affairs. After Mo Tzu's death the sect split into three groups. The words of the leaders were taken as law; before they died they chose their own successors.

The decades which separated Mo Tzu from Confucius were the beginning of one of the most turbulent and eventful periods in Chinese history, the *Chan kuo* (Warring States) period, from 403 to 221 B.C. During this time, China experienced revolutionary changes in her economy, political structure, and ideology. Advances in methods of irrigation and the growing use of iron tools in agriculture, crafts, and mining contributed to increasing prosperity and stimulated the development of trade. Cities of a size previously unknown became centers of cultural life. The archaic city-state, which had preserved the traditions of primitive democracy and the importance of personal ties, was succeeded by a centralized state governed by an impersonal bureaucratic machine. All this contributed to a situation in which tradition as such began to lose its authority. The ideas of Mo Tzu as expressed in his treatise are a vivid testimony to this fact.

*Mo Tzu* is sharply differentiated both in structure and in style from *Lun yü*. While the *Lun yü* is in dialogue form, the *Mo Tzu* (except for a few chapters) is in monologue. In essence, it is a collection of sermons, each chapter constituting a discourse on a particular theme. The most important chapters are: "Honoring the Worthy," "Universal Love," "Moderation in Expenditure," "Moderation in Funerals," "Against Music," "Against Fatalism," "Against Confucians."

Unlike the aphoristic language of the *Lun yü*, the language of the *Mo Tzu* is insipid, tedious, and tautological. It is as if Mo Tzu were anticipating a dull listener who, if he were to understand anything at all, would have to have every proposition explained to him in exhaustive detail. Here, for example, is how he proves the "harmfulness of music."

> Now the rulers and ministers, seated in their lofty towers and broad pavilions, look about them, and there are the bells, hanging like huge cauldrons. But unless the bells are struck, how can the rulers get any delight out of them? Therefore it is obvious that the rulers must have someone to strike the bells. But they cannot employ old men or young boys, since their eyes and ears are not

keen enough and their arms are not strong, and they cannot make the sounds harmonious or see to strike the bells front and back. Therefore the rulers must have young people in their prime, whose eyes and ears are keen and whose arms are so strong that they can make the sounds harmonious and see to strike the bells front and back. If they employ young men, then they will be taking them away from their plowing and planting, and if they employ young women, they will be taking them away from their weaving and spinning. Yet the rulers and ministers will have their music, though their music-making interferes to such an extent with the people's effort to produce food and clothing! Therefore Mo Tzu said: Making music is wrong.[2]

Constantly repeated references in the treatise to the teacher's words suggest the central chapters are based on the notes of his students. In several chapters devoted to questions of logic and military affairs, speeches are put into the mouths of Mo Tzu's followers. Most scholars believe that these chapters were written much later than those which set forth Mo Tzu's political, ethical, and religious views.

## Utilitarianism and universal love

The concept of "utilitarianism" is usually associated with the English philosophical school of the eighteenth and nineteenth centuries, whose main representatives were Jeremy Bentham and John Stuart Mill. But the principle formulated by these philosophers—that human actions should be evaluated according to their utility, and that the goal of action should be the greatest happiness of the greatest number—is the basic argument of a large number of ancient and contemporary thinkers. This approach is close to Mo Tzu's, with the difference that for him the scale for measuring human actions and values was not the "greatest happiness" but the satisfaction of the elementary needs of the largest number. For example, the above quotation shows that he demanded the abolition of music on these grounds.

At first glance, Mo Tzu's position does not seem very different from Confucius'. In fact, a certain coincidence of views can be discerned. Like Confucius, Mo Tzu believed that political activity has a definite meaning, and that the ruler must be concerned with improving the lot of the people. But Mo Tzu broke radically with Confucius on what should be derived from these propositions. Certain basic conclusions follow from Mo Tzu's insistence on measuring everything with the strict yardstick of "satisfaction of the needs of the greatest number." First of all, this meant a refusal to exalt family ties as did Confucius and, more particularly, the Confucians. If everything depends on how many persons have benefited from a given action, the question of who received the benefit is of secondary importance. Secondly, Mo Tzu thereby shifted the accent from quality to quantity and rejected everything related to the idea of the harmoniously developed personality. Thirdly, his concentration on questions of a mass character made the problem of organization of prime importance for the ruler. Hence, Mo Tzu's particular interest in the functioning and perfection of the state machine.

Mo Tzu's idea of universal love should be seen as a polemic against the peculiar Confucian emphasis on the family as the basic social unit. Of all Mo Tzu's ideas, that of universal love has gained the widest currency; and ever since ancient times this idea has been synonymous with Mo Tzu. Lamenting the popularity of Mo Tzu's teaching, Meng Tzu (372–289 B.C.), a follower of Confucius, said, "Mo Tzu, by preaching universal love repudiated the family." [3] At the beginning of the twentieth century it was a commonplace among European scholars that Mo Tzu was a bolder and more original thinker than Confucius, because of the contrast between Mo Tzu's "universal love" and Confucius' "private (i.e. family) love." A number of sinologists considered him a forerunner of socialism. Thus, E. Faber in his book *Grundgedanken des alten Chinesischen Sozialismus, oder Lehre des Philosophen Micius,* shows that Mo Tzu's universal love has a communistic character.[4] Alexandra David praises Mo Tzu for preaching love on the basis of social necessity rather than from any sort of sentimental motives. In her words, such a love can ensure order and social stability.[5] Missionary-sinologists also paid tribute to such views. Thus, Leon Wieger wrote that Mo Tzu was "the lone Chinese thinker of whom it can be said that he believes in God, the lone Chinese apostle of charity, and the knight of truth." [6] A. Forke also highly valued the idea of universal love, noting that Mo Tzu deserves immortality as an ethical thinker.[7] Let us see how this idea is expressed in Mo Tzu's treatise.

The point of departure is the statement that all-under-Heaven is in a state of disorder. "Great states attacking small ones, great families overthrowing small ones, the strong oppressing the weak, the many harrying the few, the cunning deceiving the stupid, the eminent lording it over the humble." [8] Searching for the reason for these misfortunes, Mo Tzu says:

> Do they come about from loving others and trying to benefit them? Surely not! They come rather from hating others and trying to injure them. And when we set out to classify and describe those men who hate and injure others, shall we say that their actions are motivated by universality or partiality? Surely, we must answer, by partiality, and it is this partiality in their dealings with one another that gives rise to all the great harms in the world. Therefore, partiality must be destroyed. . . . It must be replaced by universality.[9]

Such reasoning is quite typical of Mo Tzu. The problem of social order is discussed abstractly; man, as a real being with definite feelings, is ignored. Man is viewed as a *tabula rasa* on which anything may be written or erased. Elsewhere Mo Tzu expresses himself on this subject even more bluntly, saying that to bring about humanity and justice "one must get rid of joy and anger, pleasure and sadness, love and hatred." [10] Only through such an abstract approach, divorced from the reality of human feelings, is Mo Tzu's artificial opposition of terms possible. What exactly is the meaning of the statement that all misfortune is the result of partiality? Those authors are partly correct who say that Mo Tzu, in contrast to the Confucians, opposes the exaltation of family ties to the detriment of broader human feelings. But if in appealing for the perfection of society one can assert that family bonds are inadequate and need to be supplemented by fraternal relations with all people, it is still impossible to agree that such bonds ("partiality" in Mo Tzu's terms) must be discarded and replaced by universal love.

The initial premise of Mo Tzu's famous theory of altruism contains a concept of man which in principle is incompatible with any rational notion of love for others. The Taoist treatise *Chuang Tzu* early noted the peculiar contradiction in Mo Tzu between the declaration of universal love and the disdain for the feelings of real men which is at the basis of his world view. It not only notes that "when people sing [Mo Tzu] opposes singing, when they cry [he] opposes crying, when they are joyful [he] opposes joy" but also makes the ironic comment, "I fear that to teach people this means not to love them." [11]

The true character of "universal love" is revealed most vividly by the way in which Mo Tzu proposes to bring it about. Here we must distinguish between two methods. One of them is the attempt to convince everyone that altruism is advantageous. Here Mo Tzu unconsciously falls into the very same position of "partiality," whose abolition he has just demanded. Mo Tzu says:

> When a filial son plans for his parents, does he wish others to love and benefit them, or does he wish others to hate and injure them? It stands to reason that he wishes others to love and benefit his parents. Now if I am a filial son, how do I go about accomplishing this? Do I first make it a point to love and benefit other men's parents, so that they in return will love and benefit my parents. . . . So if all of us are to be filial sons, can we set about it any other way than by first making a point of loving and benefiting other men's parents? [12]

In such fashion "universality," returning in the direction of "partiality," loses the status of an unconditional postulate. But as a means of egoism the thesis of universal love cannot be long-lasting. Can one doubt that egoism can find more convenient and quicker acting instruments?

The second means Mo Tzu offers for implementing his ideals is of even greater interest. It consists in convincing the rulers of the advantages of "universal love."

> If the rulers really delighted in them [universal love and mutual benefit] promoted them with rewards and praise, and prevented neglect of them by punishment, then I believe the people would

turn to universal love and mutual benefit as naturally as fire turns upward or water turns downward, and nothing in the world could stop them.[13]

Thus the implementation of "universal love" is entrusted to the ruler. With the aid of rewards and punishments, he will compel those who were not persuaded by the arguments of the artful rhetorician that to love each other is most advantageous.

One element united both methods of implementing universal love—the premise that man will do only what will benefit him. Along with the ideal of the obedient son and the model subject, Confucius creates an ideal of man acting in an unselfish effort to implement moral values, but Mo Tzu is sure that man is concerned only with obtaining pleasure for himself and avoiding suffering. Mo Tzu recognizes no other motives. Leon Vandermeersch terms this a "pessimistic" conception.[14] Whether or not Mo Tzu's brisk activism can be called pessimism, Vandermeersch is right in the sense that Mo Tzu did not believe in man's better possibilities. And although he demanded maximum altruism from man, he thought that this could be achieved only through the external action on man of punishments and rewards. Because the system of punishments and rewards proceeds from the state, for Mo Tzu the basic problem is that of state organization. For Confucius, man stood in the center and politics was spoken of as the sphere of ethics, the relations of man to man, but Mo Tzu transferred the center of gravity to the state, thereby taking a vital step in the direction of politicizing Chinese social thought.

Renouncing the ideal of personality and transferring all his hopes to the ideal state, Mo Tzu creates the first Chinese utopia.

## The utopia of universal conformism

Utopian government is described in the chapter "Identifying with one's superior" (*shang t'ung*). Before discussing the contents of this chapter, it is perhaps necessary to confront the perplexity aroused in the reader by the fact that the treatise speaks of the past. As everyone knows, utopias look toward the future. The special character of utopian ideas in China is precisely that they appear in the garb of a past golden age. Etienne Balazs has taken note of this, remarking that while in the history of the West the new was also often decked out in historical costume, in China this tendency can be considered almost organic. Balazs aptly called this kind of idea a retrospective utopia.[15] Now let us see how Mo Tzu conceived of the ideal government.

He begins with a description of the condition of society before there was a government.

> In ancient times . . . one man had one view, two men had two views, ten men had ten views—the more men the more views. Moreover, each man believed that his own views were correct and disapproved of those of others, so that people spent their time condemning one another. Within the family fathers and sons, older and younger brothers grew to hate each other and the family split up, unable to live in harmony, while throughout the world people resorted to water, fire and poison in an effort to do each other injury. Those with strength to spare refused to help out others, those with surplus wealth would let it rot before they would share it, and those with beneficial doctrines to teach would keep them secret and refuse to impart them. The world was as chaotic as though it were inhabited by birds and beasts alone. To anyone who examined the cause, it was obvious that this chaos came about because of the absence of rulers and leaders.[16]

Fung Yu-lan noted that this theory, which held that a war of all against all existed until the appearance of the state, resembled that of Hobbes.[17] In the *Leviathan* Hobbes writes:

> And be there never so great a multitude; yet if their actions be directed according to their particular judgments, and particular appetites, they can expect thereby no defense, nor protection, neither against a common enemy, nor against the injuries of one another. For being distracted in opinions concerning the best use and application of their strength, they do not help but hinder one another; and reduce their strength by mutual opposition to nothing: whereby they are easily, not only subdued by a very few that agree together; but also when there is no common enemy, they make war upon each other, for their particular interests.[18]

The way out of this situation according to Mo Tzu is in the people's choosing a Son of Heaven.

Therefore the most worthy and able man in the world was selected and set up as Son of Heaven. After the Son of Heaven had
been set up, because his strength alone was insufficient, other
worthy and able men were selected from throughout the world
and installed as his three high ministers. . . . [But] because the
world was so broad, and because it was not always possible for
the ruler and his ministers alone to judge accurately what would
be right and profitable for people living in distant countries and
strange lands, the world was divided into countless states, and
feudal lords and chiefs were set up to administer them. After the
feudal lords and chiefs had been set up, because their strength
alone was insufficient, worthy and able men were chosen from
the various states to act as their officials.

   When all these officials had been installed, the Son of
Heaven proclaimed the principle of his rule to the people of the
world, saying, "Upon hearing of good or evil, one shall report it
to his superior. What the superior considers right all shall consider right; what the superior considers wrong all shall consider
wrong. If the superior commits any fault, his subordinates shall
remonstrate with him; if his subordinates do good, the superior
shall recommend them. To identify oneself with one's superior
and not to form cliques on the lower levels—such conduct as this
shall be rewarded by those above and praised by those below. If,
upon hearing of good or evil, one fails to report it to his superior;
if what the superior considers right is not accepted as right and
what the superior considers wrong is not accepted as wrong; if
his subordinates fail to remonstrate with the superior when he
commits a fault, or if the superior fails to recommend his subordinates when they do good; if the subordinates make common
cause among themselves and fail to identify themselves with their
superiors—if there is conduct such as this, it shall be punished by
those above and condemned by the people at large." The rulers
meted out their rewards and punishments on this basis, examining with the greatest care to make sure that such rewards and
punishments were just.[19]

   The significant contradiction in these statements demonstrates that Mo Tzu's theory occupies a position halfway between
that of Confucius and Legalism. Confucius demanded that the
*chün-tzu* remonstrate with the ruler. But to do this the *chün-tzu*
himself must be an autonomous moral personality, he must be in
harmony with but not identical to others. Characteristically, Con-

fucius appraised negatively the very quality of sameness, uniformity, unification (*t'ung*) which Mo Tzu praised so highly and which played such a vital role in his conception of the state. The passage quoted above leaves no room for doubt that this state is founded on the most complete conformism.[20] In this context the demand that an erring superior be corrected becomes the greatest of absurdities, for it is impossible to comprehend how one who, as it has just been said, is bound to deem correct what his superior considers correct can point out the errors of this selfsame superior. This contradiction can be resolved by supposing that Mo Tzu himself did not fully realize his rupture with Confucius' approach. Hence he used Confucian terms like *jen* (humanity), *chün-tzu*, etc. which the Legalists subsequently renounced entirely. This also explains why amidst the mechanistic system of universal agreement, denunciation, and obedience, there suddenly appeared the proposition that it is necessary to remonstrate with one's superiors, a borrowing of Confucius' teachings about the *chün-tzu*. The Legalist thinker Han Fei (280–230 B.C.) waged an open struggle against the Confucian doctrine that a true adviser is bound to remonstrate with his sovereign.[21]

Still another special feature of the text quoted above, an entirely new element in Chinese political thought, is the system of information based on denunciations which was proclaimed for the first time as a basis of government. In the *Lun yü* (chapter 13, paragraph 18) there is a dialogue conveying Confucius' attitude toward this question. There it says:

> The ruler of She said to Confucius, "In my country there are men who may be called upright. If the father of such a man steals a sheep, the son will denounce him." Confucius replied, "In my country upright men are of a different sort. A father will shield his son, a son will shield his father. This is uprightness." [22]

Unlike Mo Tzu, for whom family ties (like feelings in general) do not exist, Confucius placed these feelings above obligation to the state. On the basis of the general tenor of Confucius' teachings one may state that denunciation as a method of government generally did not meet with his approval.

To Confucius' view of government as an organism constructed on the model of a family and linked by familial feelings, Mo Tzu counterposes a view of government as a primitive machine, the identical parts of which are set into motion at the command of the ruler. Rewards and punishments are proclaimed as the universal means of governing. In essence, all the declarations of the Son of Heaven are instructions on how to operate the levers of this machine. What emerges is reminiscent of an army whose soldiers receive orders from their commander. Although an opponent of aggressive wars, Mo Tzu chooses the latter of the opposed principles of *wen* and *wu,* not only because he is a firm and irreconcilable opponent of culture, but also because in his scheme all of society is militarized. The object of Mo Tzu's appeal, the ordinary member of society, resembles a soldier even more since man is viewed as a lone individual. He is treated as a completely isolated creature who belongs to no group other than that mass in whose ranks he must perform the required duties.[23] Furthermore, we encounter here (again for the first time in the history of Chinese political thought) a complete rejection of the methods of persuasion and a switchover in governing methods to the track of compulsion.

In further developing his scheme, Mo Tzu advances along these basic lines:

> The head of each local community was the most benevolent man in the community, and when he took office, he proclaimed to the people of the community the principle of his rule, saying, "Upon hearing of good or evil, you shall report it to the town head. What the town head considers right all shall consider right; what the town head considers wrong all shall consider wrong. Leave your evil words and imitate the good words of the town head; leave your evil actions and imitate the good actions of the town head!" As long as this command was heeded, how could there be any disorder in the township?
>
> If we examine into the reason why the township was well ordered, we find that it was simply that the town head was able to unify the standards of judgement in the township, and this resulted in order.[24]

Thus everything is repeated in ascending order, from the town head to the ruler of the kingdom to the Son of Heaven.

Each of them issues an identical appeal to the people and, owing to the unification of views, achieves complete order in the territory under his jurisdiction. When one ascends to the level of the Son of Heaven, Mo Tzu declares, identification with him is not enough. One must identify with Heaven itself, lest Heaven send hurricanes and floods to the people. But the outline does not conclude on this religious note, but rather with the following declaration:

> So Mo Tzu said: In ancient times the sage kings devised the five punishments so as to bring order to the people. These were like the main thread binding a skein of silk or the main cord controlling a net, by which the sage kings bound and hauled in those among the people of the world who failed to identify themselves with their superiors. [25]

Mo Tzu's picture of the ideal unified state begins the history of Chinese utopian thought. Subsequently, when utopian ideas were taken up by the Confucian tradition as well, they continued to preserve traces of the school from which they derived. The oldest model of utopia within the Confucian canon is the plan of the "great unity" (*ta t'ung*) outlined in the small treatise *Li Yün*, a part of the collection *Li Chi*.

As noted above, this utopia relates to the past. In words ascribed to Confucius, it is said that when the Great Unity reigned, all-under-Heaven was communal property, and it was governed by the ablest and most skillful men. People treated each other as members of one family and looked on all children as their own. The aged were provided with enough to live out their full lives. The adults were provisioned with everything they needed and the young with all they required to grow up. There was food and sustenance for the childless widows, widowers, orphans, the lonely and the sick. . . . People could not bear to see the harvest rot on the ground, but they did not selfishly hurry to gather it all into their own granaries. They couldn't agree not to spend their efforts in useful labor, but they didn't wish this labor to be only for themselves. Therefore, there was neither pillage nor theft, neither brigandage nor discord, and doors were never locked. [26]

The name of this plan is similar to that of *Mo Tzu* but the contents are quite different. The exhortation to a unified conformism gives way to an appeal for mutual aid extending beyond the bounds of one's own family.

## The craft of government

When reading Mo Tzu on the state, one gets the impression of a man carried away by his discovery that the state is a machine, and delighted by the marvelous possibilities within this machine. In our analysis of Mo Tzu's utopia we stated that he sees people as parts of this machine. Clearly such an approach is antithetical to Confucius', who affirms that moral qualities alone are indispensable for governing. In the state-machine, government is a specialty, a craft like, let us say, that of the butcher. Mo Tzu says:

> If one possesses justice but not ability, ultimately there will be no way to advance along the path. This is like a carpenter who rough-hews a log, but cannot use a plumb-line. . . . Now if a *chün-tzu* were appointed to be a butcher, he would refuse since he knows not the craft, but if he were appointed a minister in the state he would agree to serve, although he cannot cope with affairs of state.[27]

In another place he compares administrators to bowyers and wheelwrights.[28] In this way technical questions of government become enormously important, particularly the problem of selecting able and skillful assistants.

How, actually, does the ruler find suitable persons? Mo Tzu suggests a simple method—instituting a system of material and moral incentives. In his opinion, the drive for success is a force sufficient even to bring about moral transformation. When the ancient kings, says Mo Tzu, declared that only the just would be given rewards, then the rich, the well-born, the king's family and intimates all decided that they too must become just. Such was the reason for their conduct. The point is that superiors can attract inferiors to their service by one means alone—material benefits. The inferiors can offer only one thing to their superiors—their ability. This is the crux of the matter.[29]

However, in addition to material incentives there is another possibility which Mo Tzu mentions: intimidation. Promoting the able and the skillful, the ancient sage-kings cashiered or demoted the unfit, reduced them to a base and impoverished position, or made slaves of them. "Thus the people, encouraged by the hope of reward and awed by the fear of punishment, led each other on to become worthy, so the worthy men increased in number and unworthy men became few." [30]

Here we can see a significant contrast with the Confucian approach to government. While Confucius is exclusively interested in the ethical side of the problem, Mo Tzu's interest is in the technical side of things. While Confucius concentrates on the goal, the primary stress here is on the means. Confucius' *chün-tzu* is unselfish. He cannot be manipulated. Mo Tzu states unambiguously that material incentive is the basic motive for the administrators' actions. He is not ashamed to say that the administrator will sell his talent for money. For Confucius, the position of a participant in government is imbued with profound dramatic intensity. For Mo Tzu it consists of the conscientious fulfillment of routine obligations.

This becomes even clearer when Mo Tzu explains how the skillful (*hsien*) should govern.[31]

> When a skillful man is given the task of ordering the state, he appears at court early and retires late, listens to lawsuits and attends to the affairs of government. As a result, the state is well-ordered and laws and punishments are justly administered. When a skillful man heads a government bureau, he goes to bed late and gets up early, collecting taxes on the barriers and markets and on the resources of the hills, forests, lakes, and fish weirs, so that the treasury will be full. As a result the treasury is full and no source of revenue is neglected. . . . When the state is well-ordered, the laws and punishments will be justly administered, the treasury will be full and the people well-off. The rulers will thus be supplied with wine and millet to use in their sacrifices to Heaven and the spirits, with hides and currency to use in their intercourse with the feudal lords of neighboring states, and with the means to feed the hungry and give rest to the weary within their realm, and to nourish their subjects.[32]

Obviously, the prosperity of the state and the well-being of the people are provided for in this case by the conscientiousness of the skilled civil servant. We should note that in the frequently recurring tautological phrases (a special feature of Mo Tzu's style), the state always figures as the prime element. Mo Tzu sees no contradiction whatsoever between the interests of the state and those of the people. This stance is directly opposed to that of Meng Tzu, who defends the interests of the people against encroachments by the rulers and, in particular, insists on the people's right to engage in fishing without taxation. Defending the interests of the state and its representatives above all, Mo Tzu establishes three principles of government:

> If the titles and positions of skillful men are not exalted enough, then the people will not respect such men; if their stipends are not generous enough, then the people will not have confidence in them; and if their orders are not enforced, then the people will not stand in awe of them.[33]

Although Mo Tzu contends that the rulers and the skillful have a mutual interest in seeking each other out, the idea that one may overthrow an unfit ruler (as Mencius proposed) or that the skillful dominate the ruler is quite alien to him. On the contrary, according to Mo Tzu, such collaboration means that the skillful sacrifice their powers on the altar of service to the ruler, and ascribe to him all their achievements.

> Thus all that was beautiful and good came to reside in the ruler, while all grudges and complaints were directed against his subordinates. Peace and joy was the portion of the ruler, care and sorrow that of his ministers. This was how the sage kings of ancient times administered their rule.[34]

This little known passage once again demonstrates that the roots of a large number of Legalist doctrines reach down to the ideology of Mo Tzu. Han Fei was very attentive to the need to hold subordinates responsible for mistakes of the ruler. He viewed the relations between the ruler and his ministers as a perpetual war, and he gave the ruler much advice on how to avoid assassination, deception and other dangers which might stem from his ministers. Although this theme is not elaborated in Mo Tzu's treatise, the essence of the passage cited—that the ruler must so employ his retainers that he gathers all the sweet fruits of his position while his ministers harvest only bitter anxieties and toil—contains this Legalist doctrine in embryonic form. At the same time, this view completely contradicts the Confucians' approach to this problem; they constantly emphasize the ruler's responsibility, and never look upon the problem of government from the perspective of "extracting pleasure from high position."

The refusal to view the ruler's activity as the discharge of a moral obligation and the view of government as a kind of craft had the further consequence that Mo Tzu introduced into the problem of government an element of quantitative calculation. One can judge how closely the ruler approaches the moral ideal only intuitively (Confucius spoke of this in a famous passage [*Analects* ch. XIII, par. 16] where he defines good government as a state where "the near approve and the distant approach"), but such judgment can never be expressed in precise mathematical form. However, as soon as governing becomes a profession, it does become possible to measure its effectiveness. At that point, a person's fitness to govern is no longer determined by whether he possesses the requisite moral qualities. Now a strict scale is used to measure those who by their knowledge and ability are fit to govern respectively a hundred, a thousand, ten thousand, etc. If one judges ability by externals without attempting to verify knowledge, says Mo Tzu, those who are not even fit to rule over a hundred are appointed to rule over a thousand; those who could not cope with a thousand are entrusted with ten thousand. Let us note his judgement of what happens in such a case.

> Now if a man who is incapable of taking charge of a thousand persons is given a post in charge of ten thousand, then he is being given a post that requires ten times what he is capable of. Affairs of government arise every day and must be attended to each day, and yet the day cannot be made ten times longer for the sake of such a man. Furthermore, it takes knowledge to attend to such affairs, but if the man's knowledge cannot be increased ten-

fold and he is still assigned to a post that requires ten times what he is capable of, then it will result in his attending to one matter and neglecting nine others. Though the man works night and day to attend to the duties of his post, it is obvious that they will never be attended to.[35]

Underlying Mo Tzu's critique of the Confucians is a sober, businesslike approach to governing which views it as a profession, and evaluates the ruler by the effectiveness of his actions rather than the degree to which he measures up to a moral ideal. One of the fatal defects of the Confucian school, in Mo Tzu's opinion, is its fatalism, its blind faith that "Long life or early death, wealth or poverty, safety or danger, order or disorder are all decreed by the Will of Heaven and cannot be modified." [36] In this connection, H. G. Creel has noted that Confucius himself never said that man was helpless before fate. Therefore it seems that one must seek to explain the reasons for Mo Tzu's critique by examining the views of Confucius' followers.[37]

However, it appears unnecessary to turn to the views of the minor Confucians in order to understand the issue. The fact is that Mo Tzu was simply a stranger to the outlook of Confucius, a man who subordinated politics to ethical values and judged the rulers by their intentions rather than by their results. As the *Lun yü* informs us, a simple man noted this view, saying of Confucius, "He's the one who 'knows it's no use, but keeps on doing it'—is that not so?" [38] The accusation that Confucianism is fatalistic and passive represents a protest of politicians against ethical norms which restrain their activity, a protest which is largely subconscious. In fact, while Mo Tzu is determined to attack culture openly, asserting that it is an "unnecessary luxury," he doesn't dare to come out against ethics. This is additional evidence that Mo Tzu's teaching stands halfway between that of Confucius and Legalism. Substituting expedience for morality and politics for ethics, he is yet somehow chary of recognizing the significance of his innovation. On the contrary, in numerous monologues he tries to prove that his teaching is the true ethics, that it alone will bring about the implementation of Confucian moral ideals.[39] Subsequently, the Legalists would derive the logical conclusions from Mo Tzu's premises, and come out openly against the principle of humanity which is "destructive to the state."

Underlying Mo Tzu's critique of the Confucians' traditionalism is an urge to remove all the obstacles which hinder the political actor.

> The Confucians say: "The superior man must use ancient speech and wear ancient dress before he can be considered benevolent." But we answer: The so-called ancient speech and dress were all modern once, and if at that time the men of antiquity used such speech and wore such dress, then they must not have been superior men. Must we then wear the dress of those who were not superior men and use their speech before we can be considered benevolent?
>
> Again the Confucians say: "The superior man should be a follower and not a maker." [40] But we answer: In ancient times Yi invented the bow, Yü invented the armor, Hsi-chung invented carts, and the craftsman Ch'iu invented boats. Do the Confucians mean, then, that the tanners, armorers, cart-makers and carpenters of today are all superior men and Yi, Yü, Hsi-chung, and the craftsman Ch'iu were all inferior men? Moreover, someone must have invented the ways which the Confucians follow, so that in following them they are, by their own definition, following the ways of inferior men.[41]

Thus Mo Tzu, the innovator, strikes a heavy blow at the traditionalism of the Confucians. But it is worthwhile to reflect on his argument. If we do we shall see that not everything is so simple and straightforward. Once more we shall see two contrasting approaches to resolving problems of social order. To the world of humanitarian culture whose values are bound up with tradition is opposed the world of the craft whose fundamental achievements derive not from the acceptance of borrowed things but from invention. While Confucians believe that in the humanitarian culture there can be nothing absolutely new, (creativity in this context largely means new interpretations, putting new contents into inherited forms [42]) the craft, on the other hand, demonstrates best of all the superiority of the new as such.

## The abolition of music

It has already been noted that Mo Tzu's universal criterion is the satisfaction of the elementary needs of the greatest number. With characteristic straightforwardness, he demands the abolition of every kind of ornamentation on these grounds. Mo Tzu demonstrates that clothes are designed only to provide warmth in cold weather and coolness in hot. Houses are for protection from thieves, from cold and wind in the winter, from heat and rain in the summer. Weapons are for protection against rebels and bandits. Boats and vehicles allow people to associate with each other. While pointing out the simple purpose of all these objects, an accompanying phrase is repeated again and again: "What is merely decorative and does not contribute to these ends should be avoided." [43] If Mo Tzu insists on moderation with respect to necessary objects, he simply demands the abolition of everything which is not intended for the satisfaction of elementary needs. His argument is contained in the chapter "Against Music."

The term *yüeh*, normally translated as "music," had a broader meaning in ancient Chinese. Usually it signified dances with musical accompaniment, but Mo Tzu interprets it even more broadly.

> Mo Tzu condemns music not because the sound of the great bells and rolling drums, the zithers and the pipes, is not delightful; not because the sight of the carvings and ornaments is not beautiful; not because the taste of the fried and broiled meats is not delicious; and not because lofty towers, broad pavilions, and secluded halls are not comfortable to live in. [44]

Thus the concept of *yüeh* included painting, carving, the culinary arts, and architecture. All these must be done away with, Mo Tzu says, because in no way do they help to ease the plight of the common people.

> There are three things the people worry about: that when they are hungry they will have no food, when they are cold they will have no clothing, and when they are weary they will have no rest. These are the three great worries of the people. Now let us try

sounding the great bells, striking the rolling drums, strumming the zithers, blowing the pipes, and waving the shields and axes in the war dance. Does this do anything to provide food and clothing for the people? [45]

Mo Tzu believes that music and dance are not only useless, but actually harmful because they divert both the common people and officials from their primary duties—production and administration. According to Mo Tzu, participation in labor distinguishes man from the beasts. Animals, birds, and insects, he says, are provided with clothing—their fur and hides. Claws are their footwear, grass and water their food and drink. Therefore, they need not labor. By contrast, man must work in order to survive.[46] From this proposition Mo Tzu concludes that human life is synonymous with labor (and with that rest which is necessary for further labor). He not only wants to destroy art and culture as useless, he also desires to destroy human feelings as well (see p. 37 above). For, as Feng Yu-lan noted, from a strictly utilitarian viewpoint, human emotions not only lack any practical value, but have no meaning whatsoever. They must be eliminated to avoid their becoming obstacles to action.[47] Man, a cog in the state in Mo Tzu's view, must not stand idle; he must be constantly in motion. Thus, concern for the lot of the masses turns into cold indifference when it comes to the real life of individual persons.

In the *Mo Tzu* are a number of interesting dialogues in which Confucians carry on polemics against Mo Tzu's approach to culture and to man. The Confucian Ch'eng Fan said to Mo Tzu: "According to you the sage-kings did not enjoy music. This is like never removing the harness from a horse, or never releasing a bow that has been drawn. This is impossible; no living creature could so endure." Mo Tzu responded that there had been music during the reign of sage-kings, but he declared that music and government had been in inverse proportion, that Yao and Shun were superior because in their reigns there was little music but much good government. The passing of time has brought more music and less good government.[48]

Kung Meng-tzu, another Confucian whose views are cited

in the *Mo Tzu*, took another tack. While in Ch'eng Fan's view man needed music because he could not live without joy, Kung Meng-tzu saw music (along with *li*, ritual) as a sign of the flowering of culture, closely linked to peace and social tranquility. Kung Meng-tzu says:

> When the country is in chaos, it should be put in order; when it is in order, ceremonials and music may be pursued. When the country is poor work should be attended to; when it is rich, ceremonials and music may be pursued.[49]

Mo Tzu replied to the Confucian:

> A country may be orderly. But it is because it is being well governed that it is orderly. . . . Now, you say, when the country is in order, ceremonials and music may be pursued. This is similar to digging a well when someone is choked and to seeking a physician when someone is dead.[50]

The contrast between the Confucian and Mohist approach to culture is vividly expressed in the passage where Mo Tzu asks a Confucian what is music necessary for. The Confucian replies, "For music's sake." Mo Tzu objects that this is like saying in response to a question "What is a house needed for?" that a house is needed for a house, while in fact a house is needed to protect against the heat in summer and the cold in winter, and to separate men and women.[51] For the Confucian, music, because of its intrinsic value, needs no justification, but Mo Tzu demands that the utility of music in satisfying elementary needs be demonstrated. He does not recognize any higher needs.

## The disappearance of Mo Tzu's school

In the fourth and third centuries B.C. the teachings of Mo Tzu enjoyed a certain popularity, but at the end of this period they suddenly vanished from the scene. In the nineteenth century, when interest in the *Mo Tzu* revived, Mohism was no longer a living doctrine, but a research subject for historians of philosophy.

Scholars offer various explanations for this sudden loss of interest in what had been an influential doctrine, a loss unique in the history of Chinese thought. Some suggest the reason was Emperor Ch'in Shih-huang's persecution of humanist culture.[52] Others see the reason as Mohist extremism, expressed in the propagation of universal love in place of all other human bonds, as well as its asceticism and demand for a strict economy.[53] Several investigators link the decline of Mo Tzu's teachings to his gloomy utilitarianism and complete absence of psychological sensitivity.[54] Burton Watson surmises that along with other features, the tedious style of the treatise played an essential role. Reading it was torment.[55]

While recognizing the importance of these factors, we think that the decisive element was the lack of cohesion in Mo Tzu's theory, which rendered it a contradictory and lifeless conglomeration. The consequence of placing the state machine on a pedestal, and attempting to ensure its greatest efficiency, was the manipulation of man through the use of punishments and rewards. When Mo Tzu referred in this context to the need to increase officials' salaries and strengthen their power, he blatantly contradicted the egalitarian tendencies of his own system, the imperative to struggle against luxury for the sake of satisfying the people's need for food and clothing. The denigration of man to the role of a cog did not accord in the slightest with the moral aspirations inherited from Confucius. Existing for a time as the ideology of a fighting sect, over the long run Mo Tzu's teaching could retain neither the allegiance of the moralist who was repelled by its utilitarianism and the mechanical quality of its utopian ideal, nor that of the true admirer of an all-powerful state who viewed its egalitarianism as essentially alien.

# CHAPTER THREE / THE THEORY AND PRACTICE OF A TOTALITARIAN STATE
## Shang Yang and Legalism

### Background to the emergence of Legalist theory

Historians who are accustomed to identifying Confucianism as the state ideology of China often forget that the first real official ideology was the doctrine of Legalism (in Chinese *fa chia*, literally "lawyers"). Confucius and Mo Tzu were unable to find a ruler who would implement their ideas. But in Shang Yang, a reformer and the founder of Legalism, we encounter someone who was even more a political activist than a theorist. In the middle of the fourth century B.C. in the far western state of Ch'in, he established through resolute measures a system which in the course of a little over a hundred years would enable the ruler of this state, Ch'in Shih-huang, to unify the entire country. Legalism was ignored by scholars for a long time, but in recent decades studies as well as translations of the classics of Legalist thought have demonstrated that this doctrine had become the chief competitor of Confucianism as early as the fourth century B.C.[1] It has also become clear that, afterward as well, Legalist influence not only rivaled Confucianism, but also determined to a significant degree both specific features of the state machine of imperial China and the thinking of its officials. Leon Vandermeersch is quite correct in asserting that throughout the entire span of Chinese history there has not been a single significant state measure which does not bear the mark of Legalist influence.[2]

In contrast to the teachings of Confucius and Mo Tzu, Legalism lacks a recognized founder. The first Chinese bibliography, the *I-wen-chih* (a section of the History of the Former Han Dynasty) says that this current of thought was created by officials who insisted on the establishment of definite rewards and strict punishments. In addition to Shang Yang, those who are usually included among the founders of Legalism are Shen Pu-hai, a political actor and thinker of the fourth century B.C., and Shen Tao, a philosopher of the fourth to third centuries B.C. Han Fei (ca. 280–230 B.C.) summed up Legalist doctrine and was its greatest theorist. The large treatise *Han Fei Tzu* is ascribed to him.

A study of Legalist works suggests that Shang Yang was, in fact, the founder of Legalism. Of the works of Shen Tao [3] and Shen Pu-hai only isolated fragments have been preserved. In recent years, however, H. G. Creel has argued that Shen Pu-hai, who developed the technique of controlling activity and testing the abilities of officials, played a role in the development of Legalism which was no less important than that of Shang Yang.[4] But this thesis lacks sufficient evidence. As for Han Fei, he tried to lay a Taoist theoretical foundation under a somewhat toned-down version of Shang Yang's political philosophy, and to supplement it with various ideas taken from Shen Pu-hai. Han Fei's basic theses are borrowed from Shang Yang, and several chapters of the *Shang-chün shu* are even reproduced in the *Han Fei Tzu* with minor changes and abbreviations.

Shang Yang lived in the fourth century B.C. during the tempestuous era of the Warring States. At this time the Chinese states were engaged in constant warfare with each other. The weakest fell prey to their powerful neighbors. Even the strongest were threatened by rebellions, uprisings, and wars. Thus Chin, which once had exercised hegemony over its neighbors, fell victim to the internecine strife of several of its noble families, and in 376 B.C. its territory was divided up among Wei, Chao, and Han. The ruin of a previously powerful state produced a tremendous impact on the rulers of China, who took its downfall as a grim warning.

Already by Confucius' time, the Chou Son of Heaven had

no real power. However, the hegemons of the other states were anxious to preserve the fiction that they were acting in accordance with the instructions of the Son of Heaven. They proclaimed the wars they waged against their neighbors to be punitive expeditions carried out to preserve the rights of the Son of Heaven and "to correct" his errant subjects. Subsequently, the situation changed drastically. The final semblance of the Chou emperors' authority vanished and, one after another, the seven rulers of the remaining states appropriated his title (*wang*) which connoted a pretension to rule over all the states of China. A life and death struggle between them became unavoidable. In this world, which lacked the notion that equal states might coexist, there was no possibility of independence as such. Each ruler had a choice between dominance and subordination. In the Warring States era, the latter meant destruction of the ruling dynasty and absorption of its national territory by its conqueror. Under such conditions the only alternative to ruin was a struggle for supremacy over one's neighbors.

In the desperate war of all against all, respect for traditional culture and allegiance to moral norms could serve only to weaken the position of the combatant. The inherited rights and privileges of the nobility were just as dangerous to the power of the rulers. After all, this very nobility had contributed to the ruin of Chin. The sovereign who wished to build a powerful and efficient army needed, in the first place, to centralize power, and concentrate all resources into his own hands. This implied a reorientation of the entire social structure from its economy through its culture, so that everything could be subordinated to the single goal of acquiring control over all-under-Heaven.

The reforms of Shang Yang were aimed at achieving this task. They were designed not as temporary measures necessary for coping with extraordinary conditions, but as the beginning of a transformation that would regenerate society once and for all. It is evident from the Legalist system set forth in the book ascribed to Shang Yang, the *Shang-chün shu* (The Book of the Ruler of Shang), that there can be no doubt about this whatsoever. Just who was Shang Yang and what does his book tell us?

There is a biography of Shang Yang in Ssu-ma Ch'ien's *Historical Records*. An aristocrat from one of the petty city-states by birth, he tried to make a career in Wei, but failed. Before he died, the prime minister of the kingdom had recommended that his sovereign either employ Shang Yang or kill him; but despite this advice the king did neither. When Hsiao Kung assumed the throne in 361 B.C. as ruler of Ch'in, he invited all the able men of China to enter his service in order to help Ch'in recover the territory it had once controlled. Shang Yang traveled to Ch'in and was received by the king. Noting that the king began to nod off when listening to speeches extolling the superiority of the ancient sage-kings and their moral perfection, Shang Yang laid before him a concrete plan of action which envisioned strengthening the country through a series of far-reaching reforms. One of the courtiers objected that in governing it was impossible to neglect the traditions, usages, and customs of the people. According to Ssu-ma Ch'ien, Shang Yang replied:

> What Lung holds is the point of view of the man-in-the-street. Ordinary people abide by the old customs and scholars are immersed in the study of what is reported from antiquity. These two kinds of people are all right for filling offices and for maintaining the law, but they are not the kind who can take part in a discussion which goes beyond the law. . . . A wise man creates laws, but a foolish man is controlled by them.[5]

Hsiao Kung, having appraised Shang Yang's intellect, resoluteness, and unceremoniousness, offered him a free hand, and soon the new laws were introduced into Ch'in. By these laws the people of the country were divided into groups of five and ten families bound by mutual guarantees.

> Whoever did not denounce a culprit would be cut in two; whoever denounced a culprit would receive the same reward as he who decapitated an enemy; whoever concealed a culprit would receive the same punishment as he who surrendered to an enemy. People who had two males or more in the family, without dividing the household, had to pay double taxes. Those who had military merit, all received titles from the ruler, according to a hierarchic ladder. Those who had private quarrels, were punished according to the severity of their offence. Great and small had to

occupy themselves, with united force, with the fundamental occupations of tilling and weaving, and those who produced a large
quantity of grain or silk, were exempted from forced labour.[6]

Several years later a whole series of new reforms supplemented the first ones. Once more a decree directed at the destruction of the large patriarchal families was confirmed. A father
and his grown sons were forbidden to reside in a single household. The administrative system was unified; weights and measures were standardized.

The general thrust of these measures is clear—centralization of government, strengthening the power of the ruler over the
people, expansion of the resources of the country and their concentration in the hands of the government. We must note an important feature of Shang Yang's activity. While insisting that the
laws be publicly proclaimed, at the same time he strictly forbade
them to be discussed. The *Historical Records* say that even those
who praised the new laws were exiled to distant regions in order
to break people of the habit of discussing these matters.[7]

These laws strengthened Ch'in and enabled Shang Yang to
launch an attack against Wei. He defeated Wei in 352 B.C. and
annexed its territories bordering Ch'in on the east. In 341 B.C. he
began a new campaign against it with the aim of securing an
opening to the Huang Ho and seizing the mountain passes. Stra-
tegically, this would secure Ch'in against invasion from the east.
When Ch'in's army approached the forces of Wei, Shang Yang
sent a message to Prince Ang, the Wei commander, in which he
alluded to the erstwhile friendship between them and wrote that
he could not bear the thought of the coming bloody battle. He offered to meet with him to conclude a peace agreement. Prince
Ang, trusting Shang Yang, accepted this invitation. During a
feast he was seized by Ch'in soldiers who were hiding in am-
bush. After this the leaderless Wei army was routed, and Wei
was compelled to cede the lands lying to the west of the Huang
Ho to Ch'in. For this victory Hsiao Kung richly rewarded Shang
Yang.

After Hsiao Kung's death in 338 B.C., Hui Wen Kung as-
cended the throne of Ch'in. The new ruler had long hated Shang

Yang and this spelled his doom. When Shang Yang learned that a warrant was out for his arrest, he fled and tried to stop overnight at a wayside inn. But the innkeeper would not let him in because, according to Shang Yang's own laws, an innkeeper who gave lodging to an unknown person was subject to severe punishment. Shang Yang fled to Wei, but Wei hated him for his traitorous seizure of Prince Ang and refused to accept him. When Shang Yang attempted to flee to a neighboring country, the people of Wei declared that he was a Ch'in rebel who must be returned to that country. In a desperate effort to save himself, Shang Yang raised an army from the district which Hsiao Kung had alloted to him and tried to attack the small state of Cheng, but the troops of Ch'in caught up with him. He was killed and his whole family exterminated.

Ssu-ma Ch'ien concludes his biography of Shang Yang with the observation:

> The Lord of Shang was naturally, in character, a hard and cruel man. When we find in his story that he tried to impress Duke Hsiao by the methods of the Emperors and Kings we may be sure that what he held forth was frivolous talk and did not represent his real nature. . . . After attaining high position he punished the tutor of the heir to the throne and betrayed the Wei general, Ang . . . from which it is clear that the Lord of Shang was a man of little favour. I have read the books on "Opening and Debarring" and on "Agriculture and War," which are in keeping with the deeds he did. There is reason enough why he should have finally left a bad reputation in Ch'in.[8]

The works cited by Ssu-ma Ch'ien appear as chapters in the *Shang-chün shu*. In addition to those chapters the book includes many others which apparently date for the most part from the fourth and third centuries B.C. As the Dutch sinologist J. L. Duyvendak—who translated the *Shang-chün shu* into English in 1928—suggested, it is highly improbable that Shang Yang, who was killed almost as soon as he went into retirement, wrote anything at all. Even a quick perusal of the book reveals that he could not be its author.[9] L. S. Perelomov, however, argues that the oldest part of the *Shang-chün shu* consists of Shang Yang's original notes.[10] It is possible that several chapters incorporate reports which Shang Yang made to the ruler.

The very structure of the *Shang-chün shu* reveals traces of Mohist influence. In contrast to the monuments of early Confucian and Taoist thought, here one finds the first attempt (after Mo Tzu) at a systematic exposition of material. One may say that the central element in both teachings—the organization of the state machine—itself dictates the need to organize the material in the form of thematic chapters. No less certain is the similarity in the rhetorical methods used by the Mohist preachers and the Legalist advisers. The atmosphere of activity and the attempt to convince one's interlocutor at all costs, which is so characteristic of both schools (the supposition is that the interlocutor is the ruler), is expressed stylistically in the use of tautologies and the importunate repetition of the basic thesis. A passage has been cited which allows the reader to become familiar with this feature of *Mo Tzu*. To give some idea of this aspect of the *Shang-chün shu*, let us present an excerpt from chapter 2 of this book, entitled "An Order to Cultivate Waste Lands."

> If music and fine clothing do not penetrate to all the districts, the people, when they are at work, will pay no attention to the latter, and when they are at rest, will not listen to the former. If, at rest, they do not listen to the one, their spirits will not become licentious, and if, at work, they pay no attention to the other, their minds are concentrated. If their minds are concentrated and their spirits are not licentious, then it is certain waste lands will be brought under cultivation.
>
> If it is impossible to hire servants, great prefects and heads of families are not supported and beloved sons cannot eat in laziness. If lazy people cannot be inactive, and hirelings do not find a livelihood, there will certainly be agriculture; when great prefects and heads of families are not supported, agricultural affairs will not suffer; and when beloved sons cannot eat in laziness and lazy people cannot be inactive, then the fields will not lie fallow. If agricultural affairs do not suffer and farmers increase their farming, then it is certain waste lands will be brought under cultivation.[11]

## The highest goal—absolute power for the ruler

Mo Tzu said that the state was a machine to be used for the general welfare. That the ruler might use this machine for himself is for him an incidental and secondary motif. The unique feature of Shang Yang's theory is his rejection, as a piece of silly naïveté, of the idea that the state machine exists to serve the people and his frank declaration that not the people but the ruler are in need of the state. And the ruler needs it above all to subordinate the people to himself, and then to use it for the conquest of hegemony in all-under-Heaven. Shang Yang says: "Of old, the one who could regulate the empire was he, who regarded as his first task the regulating of his own people; the one who could conquer the strong enemy was he, who regarded as his first task the conquering of his own people." [12]

The idea that the relations between the state and the people are antagonistic is a feature that distinguishes Legalist theory from other trends of political thought in both the East and the West. Undoubtedly there is a resemblance between Legalism and Machiavellism. The Italian thinker, like the proponents of Legalism, freed the political actor from the need to observe the norms of morality and deemed all means acceptable in the struggle for power. However, Machiavelli viewed despotic violence as a powerful political medicine, necessary for corrupt states, but certainly not as an end in itself. He viewed the republic as the ideal form of government; but in his opinion it was suited only to a free people, capable of self-government, like the ancient Romans or the Swiss. [13] Although placing the ruler above the law and morality, he by no means considered that the goal of government was the transformation of subjects into automata whom one could manipulate by means of a system of punishments and rewards. In Machiavelli there is no trace of that enthusiasm for struggling against the people which permeates the *Shang-chün shu*. While Machiavelli says the people should be strong and independent, Shang Yang says, "A weak people means a strong state and a strong state means a weak people. Therefore, a country, which has the right way, is concerned with weakening the people." [14]

The people, Shang Yang asserts, are valuable only as a tool in the hands of the ruler. "Having a numerous population, but not employing it, is like having no population." [15] This is an entirely new model for the relationship between the ruler and the people. While Confucius, viewing the state as a large family, thought that the ruler should be like an anxious father to his subjects, Shang Yang suggested that the ruler approach the people as raw material ready to be worked. "For the way in which the conquering of the people is based upon the regulation of the people, is like the effect of smelting in regard to metal or the work of the potter in regard to clay." [16]

The Legalists particularly stressed the need to employ strict criteria. The *Shang-chün shu* says:

> The early kings hung up scales with standard weights, and fixed the length of feet and inches, and to the present day these are followed as models, because their divisions were clear. Now dismissing standard scales and yet deciding weight, or abolishing feet and inches and yet forming an opinion about length, even an intelligent merchant would not apply this system, because it would lack definiteness. . . . Therefore, the ancient kings understood that no reliance should be placed on individual opinions or biased approval, so they set up models and made the distinctions clear. Those who fulfilled the standard were rewarded, those who harmed the public interest were punished. The standards for rewards and punishment were not wrong in their appraisals and therefore people did not dispute them. [17]

The *Han Fei Tzu* notes that the ancient sage king Yao could no more have ruled the state without laws than the famous carpenter Hsi Chung could have made the wheel by relying on his vision alone without the use of the compass and T-Square. [18]

Like Confucius, Meng Tzu stressed the obligations of the father-ruler toward his children-subjects whom he must instruct and teach and whose welfare he must concern himself with, resorting to compulsion only in extreme cases. Meng Tzu said that when the ruler no longer behaves like a father but turns into a tyrant, the subjects have the right to rise up, overthrow and kill him like a common bandit. [19] But it need hardly be said that if the ruler is a craftsman who must measure his material accurately in order to transform it into a useful object, it is out of the question for the material with which the ruler works—his subjects—to possess any right to object to the means applied to them. Such an objection would be as unthinkable as a piece of wood protesting against being sawed, planed, cut, and polished. The early Confucians began with the notion that in politics everything depends in the final analysis on human relations. For the Legalists, however, human personality vanishes completely. In place of it there appears, on the one hand, an active person stripped of all human qualities except the will to power, and on the other hand, the material of his activity, the mass among whom human faces can no longer be distinguished.

The entire corpus of Legalist works embodies a systematic struggle against the Confucian concept of the autonomous human personality. Inheriting Mo Tzu's view of man either as an animal who can be manipulated with the carrot and the stick—the system of punishments and rewards—or as a cog in the state machine, Shang Yang says, "Shame and disgrace, labour and hardship are what the people dislike; fame and glory, ease and joy are what the people pay attention to" [20] and "It is the nature of the people . . . [to] strive for gain." [21] This same thought is repeated numerous times in *Han Fei Tzu*. Han Fei indicates that even in the relations between parents and children, considerations of advantage are dominant. He writes, "When a son is born the parents congratulate each other, but they kill the daughters. . . . The parents think of future comforts and calculate long-term benefits." [22] Consequently, says Shang Yang, developing this same thought, the government can get people to do what it encourages and refrain from what it punishes. [23] It can create conditions that will force even villains and robbers to abide by its rules or, on the contrary, make even good people commit crimes. [24]

Thus, everything depends not upon the qualities of the human personality, but on the position which a person occupies and which alone enables him to achieve his desired goal—one-man rule. [25] Given such an approach, the first priority becomes the development of methods required to attain this goal. Since the strength of the state is inseparably linked to the weakness of the people, these methods lead inevitably to the weakening of the people.

## How to secure absolute power?

The most important method of governing, Shang Yang argues, should be law (*fa*). To understand the meaning Shang Yang and his followers gave to this term we must carefully examine the derivation and essence of this concept.

I noted above that Confucius opposed publication of the laws. Believing that successful government depended exclusively on the moral qualities of the leader, he asserted that penal laws (and these were the form of the oldest legislation in China) were not necessary and could only bring harm. The *Lun yü* cites a saying of Confucius:

> Govern the people by regulations, keep order among them by chastisements, and they will flee from you, and lose all self-respect. Govern them by moral force, keep order among them by ritual, and they will keep their self-respect and come to you of their own accord.[26]

The typical Confucian emphasis on the moral aspect of the problem leads to an uncompromising rejection of uniform rules of punishment and to the propagation of government based on educating the people in the spirit of traditional virtues.

Confucius' moral approach was alien to Mo Tzu, who restored punishments as one of the basic means of governing. Combined with rewards, they allow the ruler to manipulate man on the basis of his inherent passions—on the one hand, the striving for pleasure; on the other, fear. Here, as in other parts of their program, the Legalists were Mo Tzu's heirs. They armed themselves with the method of rewards and punishments as the dominant means of governing and gave this method the name of *fa* (law). In several ancient sources the term *fa* had appeared in this sense, but for the most part it had acquired a different meaning—that of "model" or "standard"—by the fourth century B.C.[27] It was no accident that the Legalists chose to use precisely this term in the sense of a system of rewards and punishments. It embodied their claim that henceforth the only norm of conduct would be the law of the state, which would determine punishments and rewards. Law must become the regulator of human action, replacing all traditions of morality and culture.

Legalist law also had no relation to religion. Noting that it represented a code of rules suited for the centralizing and expansionist goals of the government, Duyvendak writes:

> It was the expression of the state's own growing self-consciousness. It is very remarkable that, when we find the necessity for publishing the laws urged, it is not, as elsewhere, an expression of the popular wish to safeguard the people's rights and privileges for the future; on the contrary, it is the government itself that desires their publication as a safeguard of its own power, as it expects that the laws will be better observed, if people know exactly what punishments the non-observance will entail.[28]

This concept of law, devoid of all moral and religious sanctions, is unique in world history. In ancient Greece, Judea, and the Islamic countries, a divine provenance was ascribed to law. During almost the entire span of Indian history, with the exception of a short period of Ashoka's rule, the religious basis of law was an indisputable dogma.

> The contrast of the Chinese attitude to the belief in a divine origin of the law is indeed striking, for in China no one at any time has ever hinted that any kind of written law—even the best written law—could have had a divine origin.[29]

Further developing Mo Tzu's notion of the state as a machine, the Legalists use terms taken from the technical sphere. Rewards and punishments are seen as two handles which the ruler may use to govern effectively and achieve power and authority.[30] But the role of these handles is far from equal. Again and again the Legalists stress that punishment is the main handle, while rewards are ancillary. The *Shang-chün shu* says:

> In countries that attain supremacy, there is one reward to nine punishments, and in dismembered countries, nine rewards to every one punishment.[31]

Elsewhere this thought is expressed more fully and in somewhat different form:

> In a country that has supremacy, there are nine penalties as against one reward; in a strong country, there will be seven pen-

alties to three rewards and in a dismembered country, there will be five penalties to five rewards.[32]

Han Fei echoes Shang Yang:

> If punishments prevail the people will be peaceful. But if there is an abundance of rewards, villainies will multiply.[33]

Thus there must be far more punishments than rewards. Moreover, in Shang Yang's words, the rewards must be light and the punishments heavy.

> The fact that penalties are heavy makes rank the more honorable, and the fact that rewards are light makes punishment the more awe-inspiring.[34]

Such predominance of punishments is expressed in the following way in several passages of the *Shang-chün shu:*

> If you wish to imitate the ancients, you will have orderly government by promoting virtue, and if you wish to imitate modern times, you will have laws by emphasizing punishments.[35]

Another passage expresses this even more precisely:

> If you govern by punishment the people will fear. Being fearful, they will not commit villainies.[36]

In Han Fei's opinion, the ruler would commit a great error were he to seek to mitigate punishments.

> Hence no release from the death penalty, no remission of punishment. Both release from the death penalty and remission of punishment, being called "authority-losing" on the part of the ruler, mark the fall of the Altar of the Spirits of Land and Grain into danger.[37]

The Legalist concept of the salutary role of strict punishments is well-illustrated in a story from the *Shang-chün shu*. Duke Wen, the ruler of Ch'in, ordered the punishment of his close associate, who had arrived late to a meeting dealing with the question of punishment. This penalty supposedly sent everybody else into such a state of trepidation that in the wars which ensued, soldiers dared not disobey in the slightest, and the state of Ch'in gained several victories in a row. The story concludes with the following observation: "Thus Duke Wen, relying on strict punishment for a light crime, caused the state of Ch'in to enjoy order." [38]

But although intimidation was the basic means of governing in the Legalist state, the use of rewards existed alongside it. What kinds of rewards and what role was allotted to them in the Legalist system of rule? The answers to these questions are found in the passage of the *Shang-chün shu* referring to the encouragement of denunciations.

> If punishments are applied to accomplished crimes, then villainy will not be banished . . . Therefore, in the case of one who wishes to attain supremacy, punishments have to be applied at the intent to sin, . . . and rewards are bestowed on the denunciation of villainy, so that minor misdeeds will not escape unnoticed. [39]

Shang Yang adds, "This is my way of reverting to virtue through the death penalty and of combining justice with violence." [40]

That government should be based on information received from informers was first expressed in Mo Tzu's utopian scheme. Shang Yang breathed life into this idea by rewarding informers and establishing punishments for failure to inform. Subsequently, Han Fei voiced his approval of relying on informers. He conducted an open polemic with Confucius in connection with the dialogue in the *Lun yü* between Confucius and the ruler of She on the question of who should be considered an upright man. Insisting that law is incompatible with humaneness and justice, Han Fei wrote:

> Of old, there was in the Ch'u State a man named Chi-kung. Once his father stole a sheep, wherefore he reported to the authorities. Thereupon the prefect said, "Put him to death," as he thought the man was loyal to the ruler but undutiful to his father. So that man was tried and executed. From this it can be seen that the honest subject of the ruler was an outrageous son of his father. [41]

Despite the enormous influence of Legalist theory on the legislation of imperial China, it is interesting to note that beginning with the Han period legislation adhered to the Confucian principle of placing family ties before obligations to the state. The close relatives of a criminal could hide him with impunity (as long as it was not a question of "treason" or "rebellion") and were not required to testify against him in court.[42]

Rewards were used to encourage military exploits as well as denunciations. The seventeenth chapter of the *Shang-chün shu*, titled "Rewards and Punishments," stresses this aspect and says, "War and nothing else should open the gates to riches and honors." [43] In this case:

> the strong devote themselves to warfare, the old and feeble devote themselves to defense; for those who die, there is no regret and the living are bent on exerting themselves. . . . The desire of people for riches and honour does not generally cease before their coffins are closed, and when the gate to riches and honour has its approach in soldiering, then, when people hear of war, they congratulate each other and whether at work or at rest, at times of drinking or eating, they will sing songs of war.[44]

The *Han Fei Tzu* provides additional information about this point of Shang Yang's program, saying that according to Shang Yang's laws with every severed head an additional step upward was taken on the career ladder. Although Han Fei was generally an enthusiastic partisan of Shang Yang, he criticized this particular measure. He wrote:

> Thus promotion in office and rank is equivalent to the merit in head-cutting. Now supposing there were a law requesting those who cut off heads in war to become physicians and carpenters, then neither houses would be built nor would diseases be cured. Indeed carpenters have manual skill; physicians know how to prepare drugs; but, if men are ordered to take up these professions on account of their merits in beheading, then they do not have the required abilities. Now governmental service requires wisdom and talent in particular; beheading in war is a matter of courage and strength. To fill government offices which require wisdom and talent with possessors of courage and strength, is the same as to order men of merit in beheading to become physicians and carpenters.[45]

Thus on the basis of practical considerations, the more moderate Legalist corrects the extreme Legalist.

Several scholars have argued that Legalist law shared with the contemporary sense of legality the fact that it bound the ruler to the same degree as the subject, and thus to a certain extent could act as a barrier against arbitrariness. Duyvendak, who links the universalism of the law to the fact that it was published for the information of all, partially shares this opinion.[46] An investigation of the Legalist writings as well as the history of those kings and emperors inclined toward Legalism reveals the error of this view. Legalist law was intended to serve the despot, not to limit him. In their polemics with the Confucians the Legalists put forward the idea that laws change with the times. This was a splendid theoretical basis for replacing laws that proved embarrassing to the despot with new ones.[47] Leon Vandermeersch, noting this peculiar feature of Legalist "law," sought to explain why the Legalist did not place the law above the ruler:

> The state is a machine which has no meaning in and of itself. It derives its meaning only from functioning in the service of some higher goal. Not realizing that the public good or the fatherland can be such a goal, the Legalists continued to center the state around the prince. The Legalists did not understand what the fatherland or the public good is, because the development of political ideas in China . . . was not the fruit of a liberation movement, capable of creating higher political values.[48]

According to the Legalist conception the law is a basic weapon which the ruler wields in order to secure absolute power and create a centralized and powerful state, possessed of an army poised for aggression and ready to struggle to achieve hegemony in all-under-Heaven. Both "handles" of the law serve these ends. Punishments which inexorably overtake anyone who disobeys the king's orders—be he a high official, a minister, or a commoner—are particularly well suited to a struggle against the aristocracy, the chief enemy of the ruler grappling for absolute rule. At the same time they enable the ruler to use reprisals demagogically against his own close associates in order to garner popularity with the people. Rewards, however, are a means of creating an apparatus of new people beholden to the ruler for their advancement, in place of the old apparatus consisting of "unreliable" representatives of the aristocracy. But Shang Yang would not have been a political realist had he confined himself to generalities about the need to use the handles of punishments and rewards and not offered concrete measures that would guide the ruler to his goal.

He viewed the "unification of the people" and its consolidation into two basic occupations—agriculture and the military—as particularly important. As has been noted, the concept of unification was put forward by Mo Tzu, who in various places used the very same character *i* (literally, "one," "to unite," "unity"), which later played such an essential role in the *Shang-chün shu*. Shang Yang stressed that the people, employed as they were in agriculture and the military—occupations the Legalists thought reinforced each other—would easily submit to government based on rewards and punishments and "may be used abroad." [49] He ascribed an almost magical significance to unification, single-mindedness of the people:

> A state where uniformity of purpose has been established for one year will be strong for ten years; where uniformity of purpose has been established for ten years it will be strong for a hundred years; where uniformity of purpose has been established for a hundred years it will be strong for a thousand years, and a state which has been strong for a thousand years will attain supremacy. [50]

The most important means of achieving unification was the opening up of wastelands. In chapter 2 of the *Shang-chün shu*, which is devoted to this question especially, it is said that the entire life of the country should be subordinated to the task of opening up wastelands. Thus, for example, if merchants and peasants should be forbidden to buy and sell grain, they will get no special joy from good years or large profits from famine years. They will become fearful, unsure, and finally will wish to become peasants once more so that "it is certain wastelands will be brought under cultivation." [51]

In this chapter the refrain "it is certain wastelands will be brought under cultivation" is repeated many times. It concludes the description of the most varied projects, many of which apparently are unrelated to this question. A passage was cited above in which it is stated that music and fine clothing should not be allowed into the villages. Then peasants at work would not pay attention to clothes, and at rest would not listen to music. Consequently, they would not turn out to be depraved or pampered; they would concentrate only on their work, and "it is certain that wastelands will be brought under cultivation." [52] All the hostelries along the roads must be abolished. Then, trouble-makers, conspirators and those who disturb the tranquility of the peasantry could not travel about. Innkeepers deprived of their means of livelihood would be forced to become peasants and "it is certain wastelands will be brought under cultivation." [53] High officials, too, should be forbidden to travel:

> If they stop travelling then the farmers will have no opportunity to hear of changes. . . . This being so, clever farmers will have no opportunity to discard old ways, and stupid farmers will not become clever, nor will they become fond of study, and they will apply themselves energetically to agriculture.[54]

Thus, unification is incompatible with education. In essence it amounts to the stupefaction of the people.

## The struggle against culture

Shang Yang argues that a dull and ignorant population is a source of great strength, for if the people are ignorant and have no idea of what lies beyond the confines of their village, they will have no alternative but to cultivate the soil. Shang Yang says, "When the people do not hold agriculture cheap, the country will be peaceful and free from peril." [55] He attacks with greatest fury those who distract the people with education—the Confucians who teach ancient history and poetry, and follow codes of conduct not approved from above. The frenzied anger that surfaces in the *Shang-chün shu* as soon as culture and education are mentioned is clear evidence of the broad diffusion of education in the fourth century B.C., and its attractiveness to large numbers of people. Even if one discounts the hyperbolic style of the treatise, can one consider as anything but a complaint the assertion that "all the people within the territory change and become fond of sophistry, take pleasure in study"? [56] and "Though there may be a bundle of the Odes and History in every hamlet and a copy in every family, yet it is useless for good government"? [57]

The struggle against education (which the Legalists waged simultaneously with the struggle against morality) was here merged with a struggle against the people. The *Shang-chün shu* says:

> Sophistry and cleverness are an aid to lawlessness; rites and music are symptoms of dissipation and licence; kindness and benevolence are the foster-mother of transgressions; employment and promotion are opportunities for the rapacity of the wicked. If lawlessness is aided, it becomes current; if there are symptoms of dissipation and licence, they will become the practice; if there is a foster-mother for transgressions, they will arise; if there are opportunities for the rapacity of the wicked, they will never cease. If these eight things come together the people will be stronger than the government; but if these eight things are non-existent in a state, the government will be stronger than the people. If the people are stronger than the government, the state is weak; if the government is stronger than the people, the army is strong.[58]

Arguing that it behooves the ruler to concentrate on strengthening the country's military might, and that he faces no greater danger than aspiring to knowledge and intercourse with educated people, Shang Yang says:

> When a ruler loves their sophistry and does not seek for their practical value, then the professional talkers have it all their own way, expound their crooked sophistries in the streets, their various groups become great crowds, and the people, seeing that they succeed in captivating kings, dukes and great men all imitate them. Now if men form parties, the arguments and discussions in the country will be of confusing diversity; the lower classes will be amused and the great men will enjoy it, with the result that among such a people farmers will be few and those, who, in idleness, live on others will be many. . . . land will be left lying fallow. If study becomes popular, people will abandon agriculture and occupy themselves with debates, high-sounding words and discussions on false premises; . . . people will seek to surpass one another with words. Thus the people will become estranged from the ruler and there will be crowds of disloyal subjects. This is a doctrine which leads to the impoverishment of the state and to the weakening of the army.[59]

What is being stressed here is that education distracts people from agriculture—an occupation necessary for strengthening the military power of the country. In other places, the *Shang-chün shu* emphasizes that education undermines the foundations of the state because it teaches people to think independently and pronounce independent judgments about governmental affairs. Shang Yang says of the actual liquidation of education:

> What I mean by the unification of education is that all those partisans of wide scholarship, sophistry, cleverness, good faith, integrity, rites and music, and moral culture, whether their reputations are unsullied or foul, should for these reasons not become rich or honoured, should not discuss punishments, and should not compose their private views independently and memorialize their superiors.[60]

Confucius was the first person in China to found a private school and actually introduce education independent of the political authorities. Confucius believed that the *chün tzu* not only was not obligated to carry out any order of the ruler, but must oppose the ruler when he acted unjustly. Mo Tzu, who proposed a utopia of universal conformism, turned out to be, despite himself, a successor of Confucius on this very point because he insisted that a subordinate admonish his superior if the latter committed mistakes. By branding as criminal any opinion which did not accord with dictates from above, Shang Yang tried to return Chinese society to a pre-Confucian condition.

With a thorough consistency, characteristic of totalitarian thought, Shang Yang demands a complete end to education. Comparing scholars who "live idly on others" to locusts who appear only at long intervals, but deprive the people of food for many years to come,[61] he says: "If there are a thousand people engaged in agriculture and war, and only one in the Odes and History, and clever sophistry, then those thousand will all be remiss in agriculture and war." [62] To cope with this evil, he advises the wise sovereign who has brought about unification to eliminate the useless and turn all the "scholars and dissolute people" into farmers.[63]

In essence, the Legalist approach to culture represented a continuation of Mo Tzu's approach. The difference between them was that Mo Tzu rejected culture as useless, while the Legalists held that it was not simply useless, but actually harmful to the state. It is worth noting that while Mo Tzu attacked specific aspects of culture, he did not dare to come out openly against the principle of culture itself. In the *Mo Tzu* there is a chapter entitled "Against Music," but there is no chapter entitled "Against Culture." The Legalists took this final step. *Han Fei Tzu* shows that the Legalists themselves were aware of this continuity and, although they criticized some of Mo Tzu's views, they warmly applauded his approach to culture. In the thirty-second chapter of *Han Fei Tzu* the King of Ch'u asks one T'ien Chiu why Mo Tzu was not eloquent. T'ien Ch'u replies, "If his words were eloquent, people would find their style (*wen*) pleasing, and they would forget about their validity (*chih*). Thus, "Beautiful style damages utility." [64]

Two more anecdotes may help elucidate this idea. One of them tells of a merchant who sold pearls. He placed the pearls in beautiful boxes decorated with gems. Then the buyers began to take the boxes but return the pearls. In this manner the principle of *wen* is compared with a setting which had no relation to the pearl (utility). The temptation of beauty is here proclaimed as a serious danger which one must constantly be on the lookout for.[65]

The second anecdote expresses this thought by the example of a wooden kite which Mo Tzu labored over for three years but which was smashed on its first flight. Responding to the consoling words of his pupils, who were extolling his craftsmanship, Mo Tzu says: "I am not as skilful as the maker of the cross-bar for yoking the oxen. . . . [he] spends less than one morning while the bar can pull the burden of thirty piculs, has the strength for going a long way, and lasts for a number of years." [66]

This example expresses the Mohist-Legalist approach to culture even more graphically. In both cases culture is compared to an unnecessary setting, a luxury item, but in the second anecdote, utility appears not in the form of pearls, but of a simple and crude device.

But Mo Tzu and the Legalists had differing approaches to culture. While in Mo Tzu's view all efforts were to be directed toward satisfying the essential needs of the people, Shang Yang's aim was to establish the ruler's absolute power and ensure militarization of the state for the seizure of all-under-Heaven. Therefore, despite their common hostility toward culture, the basic objectives of their criticism were not identical. Mo Tzu, who stood for economy, directed his main attack against music as a form of cultural activity which required the most "nonproductive" expenditures. Shang Yang, however, attacked the culture of the Word, above all. Apolitical music bothered him very little, but he viewed the Word as the worst enemy of militarization and despotism, which depend upon the stupidity and ignorance of the people. Repeatedly emphasizing that the Word represents a grave danger for a despotic regime, Shang Yang says, "an intelligent ruler understands that by fondness of Words one cannot strengthen the army nor open up the land." [67] This panicky fear of the Word on the part of the ideologist of despotism confirms the observation of D. Granin that an articulate individual is a threat to an autocratic regime.[68]

## Militarism

The role of war in Legalist doctrine has already been sufficiently characterized. The very contrast between the principles of *wen* and *wu* appearing in the first half of the first millennium B.C. gave rise to the thought that bellicosity and love of culture are by nature opposites. In the *Shang-chün shu* this antithesis leads to an extreme antagonism. The negative attitude toward the principle of *wen* is expressed by the reference to elements of this concept as "lice." By "lice" Shang Yang means ancient poetry, history, the rules of decorum and music, as well as humaneness, justice, good, self-perfection, sincerity, trust, eloquence, intellect.[69] The *Shang-chün shu* says again and again that if these "lice" are present in the state, then there will be no one for the ruler to employ in agriculture and the military. The final outcome will be the defeat and breakup of the state.

A quotation from the *Mo Tzu*, cited above, records the assertion by a Confucian that if the state is tranquil and at peace, then people will enjoy music. Culture in general, which flourishes in peacetime, is represented in this case by music. Shang Yang, too, recognizes the close bond between culture and peace, but he draws a different conclusion. Since culture, along with morality, poses the greatest threat, war must be waged not only to achieve hegemony but also to prevent the development of culture.

> If the country is strong and war is not waged, the poison will be carried into the territory; rites and music and the parasitic functions will arise and dismemberment will be inevitable. But if the country (being strong) thereupon wages war, the poison will be carried to the enemy, and, not suffering from rites and music and the parasitic functions, it will be strong.[70]

The notion that war itself strengthens the state by serving as an obstacle to the development of culture is expressed even more clearly in another passage:

> If a state, when poor, applies itself to war, the poison will originate on the enemy's side, and it will not have the six parasites, but will certainly be strong. If a state, when rich, does not apply itself to war, the poison is transferred to its own interior, and it will have the six kinds of parasites and will certainly be weak.[71]

Here Legalism appears as the classic ideology of war. And it is within the army that the principles of governing through a system of rewards and punishments, later proclaimed by the Legalists as the sole method of ruling society in general, are first worked out. (The army is the oldest type of organization constructed on the basis of unquestioning submission to commands.) The Legalists could accept and rework Mo Tzu's ideas because the latter's utopia itself was very reminiscent of an army. Ssu-ma Ch'ien sensed this bond between Legalism with its rewards and punishments and the principle of *wu*. He has King

Wu say that he will preserve the glory of his ancestors with the help of rewards and punishments.[72] One of the forerunners of Shang Yang was Wu Ch'i, who was successful in having the laws strictly enforced, centralizing power, and unifying public opinion.[73] In several ancient Chinese writings Shang Yang himself is depicted as a general.[74]

## The polemic between the Legalists and the Confucians

The reader may have noticed that the Legalist theory put forth by Shang Yang is the exact antithesis of early Confucianism. The goals the founders of these doctrines held, the means they proposed for reaching their goals, and their initial premises are diametrically opposed as well. In the opinion of several scholars, the absence of any common ground excluded the very possibility of dispute. For example, Burton Watson writes that the meaning and values the representatives of the two schools attached to such fundamental principles as virtue and law were so much at odds that "their arguments never so much as make contact, but simply whirl about in space like fiercely opposing windmills." [75]

An examination of ancient Chinese sources disproves this assertion. Life itself threw the Legalists and the early Confucians together. The Legalists were political actors, while the Confucians, as professional teachers and preachers, tried to influence the rulers and encourage them to implement Confucian ethical principles. Since both therefore appealed to the same rulers, they had to come up with answers to the arguments of their opponents.

This polemic can be traced back to the appearance of Legalism in the middle of the fourth century B.C. We have already taken note of the sharply polemical character of the *Shang-chün shu*. The first of the Confucian treatises that attempts to answer the ideologists of despotism is the *Meng Tzu*. Confucius, of course, also clashed with the despots and oppressors, but in his time there were not yet any ideological justifications of despotism. Therefore when Confucius called on the ruler to adopt a benevolent stance toward the people, he did not meet a direct rebuff but was simply ignored. By the fourth and third centuries B.C., a different situation had developed. An open ideological struggle against Confucian principles began. Meng Tzu has in mind the ideological opponents of the humanist approach to politics when he says: "To disown in his conversation propriety and righteousness is what we mean by doing violence to oneself. To say, 'I am not able to dwell in benevolence or pursue the path of righteousness,' is what we mean by throwing oneself away." [76]

What was Meng Tzu's reply to the Legalists? His argument varied with his audience. To his pupils he said that the gentleman should not aspire to rule all-under-Heaven, because this is not the highest value. Such a man desires only that his near ones live and prosper, that he need have no shame before Heaven or mankind, and that he may find capable pupils to educate and instruct. [77] But such a position, needless to say, could hardly be attractive to a ruler, so Meng Tzu offered a thesis obviously designed to appeal to the sovereign seeking to establish his hegemony. Directly addressing him, he argued that this goal could be achieved only along the path of humane government (*jen cheng*). *Meng Tzu* offered several definitions of such government. In one source it is described as bringing peace to the people; [78] in another, as defending the people—that is, ensuring their means of livelihood so they may support their parents and children. [79] Since for the peasants this means land, Meng Tzu worked out a detailed procedure for allotting land to them (the so-called *"ching-t'ien"* or well-field system.) [80]

In a third passage, Meng Tzu insisted that the ruler's task is to help the poor. In order to do this, the ruler must have "a heart which cannot bear human suffering." [81] The legendary ruler Yü, who thought that if someone in all-under-Heaven drowned he was the cause, had such a heart. [82] Benevolent government includes giving up military adventures, [83] mitigating punishments, lowering taxes and assessments, not establishing governmental monopolies of natural resources, caring for widows, orphans and the childless, safeguarding the traditional salary of officials. [84] If all these measures were carried out, Meng Tzu thought there would be such unity and moral force among the people that no attack need be feared. To Hui Wang of Wei, who complained of his defeats in battle, Meng Tzu replied: "If one rules the people benevolently, they will wield their sticks to oppose the strong mail and sharp weapons of the troops of Ch'in and Ch'u." [85] Meng Tzu was convinced that the benevolent ruler would also be assured of victory in battle because the people of the state against which he was fighting would come over to his side: "If a man can give full development to the feeling which makes him shrink from injuring others, it will be impossible to defeat a benevolent person such as this." [86] Therefore he proclaimed that the basic political virtue was revulsion toward killing.

*Meng Tzu* cites a conversation between Meng Tzu and Hsiang Wang of Liang. The King asks how one can establish good order in all-under-Heaven:

> I replied, "Order will be established by having it united under one sway."
> The king asked, "Who can so unite it?"
> I replied, "He who has no pleasure in killing men can so unite it."
> "Who can give it to him?" asked the king.
> I replied, "All the people of the empire unanimously will give it to him. Does Your Majesty understand the way of the growing grain? During the seventh and eighth months, when drought prevails, the plants become dry. Then the clouds collect densely in the heavens, they send down torrents of rain, and the grain erects itself, as if by a shoot. When it does so, who can keep it back? Now among the shepherds of men throughout the empire, there is not one who does not find pleasure in killing men. If there were one who did not find pleasure in killing men, all the people in the empire would look towards him with outstretched necks. Such being indeed the case, the people would flock to him, as water flows downwards with a rush, which no one represses." [87]

Meng Tzu could not imagine that a villain might rule all-under-Heaven: "There are instances of individuals without benevolence who have got possession of a single state, but there has been no instance of a person without benevolence getting possession of a whole empire." [88] Such optimism was not confirmed by events.

Not quite seventy years after Meng Tzu's death China was unified by one of the cruelest despots in world history—Ch'in Shih huang-ti.

Another famous Confucian thinker, Hsün Tzu (ca. 298–238 B.C.), treated this problem somewhat differently. While Meng Tzu argued that benevolence was the sole path to power, Hsün Tzu, who was more of a realist, envisioned three possible ways of annexing the neighboring kingdoms—by virtue, strength, or wealth. Although all three methods can achieve the goal, the most effective and economical is virtue. Forcibly annexing a settled territory means the people there must be kept in a state of fear. This requires a large garrison, which entails increased expenditures and the subsequent weakening of the country. Acquiring a new territory through wealth means that one must feed the starving population because only their hope for food binds them to the conqueror. "In such a case, you will have to issue supplies of grain from your storehouses in order to feed them, hand out goods and wealth to enrich them, and appoint conscientious officials to look after them." [89] In the final analysis, once more the country and the army will be weakened. Only by annexing a new territory through virtue may one increase the number of loyal and reliable subjects, and add unprecedented strength to the state and the army. But Hsün Tzu shared Meng Tzu's belief that only a virtuous ruler could unify China. He thought that there was a direct relationship between the size of a territory and the moral quality of the person who headed a country. "A petty man using petty methods can seize a small state and hold power over it without much strength. But all-under-Heaven is great and, unless a man is a sage, he cannot take possession of it." [90]

The Confucian ideal of benevolent government provoked a sharp response from the Legalist thinker, Han Fei Tzu. He argues that helping the poor and the indigent is not only senseless but harmful:

> When the scholars of today discuss good government, many of them say, "Give land to the poor and destitute so that those who have no means of livelihood may be provided for." Now if men

start out with equal opportunities and yet there are a few who, without the help of unusually good harvests or outside income, are able to keep themselves well-supplied, it must be due either to hard work or to frugal living. If men start out with equal opportunities and yet there are a few who, without having suffered from some calamity like famine or sickness, still sink into poverty and destitution, it must be due either to laziness or to extravagant living. The lazy and extravagant grow poor; the diligent and frugal get rich. Now if the ruler levies money from the rich in order to give alms to the poor, he is robbing the diligent and frugal and indulging the lazy and extravagant. If he expects by such means to induce the people to work industriously and spend with caution, he will be disappointed.[91]

In place of the early Confucian approach to politics based on human feelings, Han Fei offers a perspective in which all considerations that lie outside the bounds of political expediency are swept away. The confrontation between these approaches is even clearer when Han Fei opposes Meng Tzu's argument that the ruler must gain the love of the people. Insisting that the only thing needed for government is political skill, Han Fei compares the people to a stupid child who doesn't know what is good or bad for him. The ruler is like a physician who causes a temporary pain in order to cure his patient.[92]

This comparison between the people and an irresponsible child deserves our careful attention. It reflects a tradition, stemming from Mo Tzu, which views politics as a specialty requiring knowledge and specific experience. Since the common man lacks these qualities, he must turn over the task of governing to those who understand such matters. It should also be understood that this position represents a definite modification of Shang Yang's openly misanthropic position. While the latter says frankly that the ruler aspires to victory over the people, Han Fei prefers to portray the cruelty of the Legalist ruler as a salutary strictness which benefits the people themselves in the final analysis. However, one should not exaggerate the importance of these divergences. In the first place, other passages of Han Fei Tzu speak of the antithetical interests of the ruler and the people in very much the same vein as Shang Yang. Secondly, to compare the people to children is no more useful as a means of restricting the power of a despot than likening them to raw material which is worked by the craftsman.

At this point, Han Fei's approach is very close to Plato's, who frequently compares politics to medicine and says that most people's relationship to their rulers is like that of the patient to the physician.[93] In Aristotle's *Politics* we come across an interesting reply to this analogy, which is aimed at democrats who believe that adults are capable of resolving their own problems. Setting forth Plato's theory, Aristotle writes:

> Hence according to this argument the masses should not be put in control over either the election of magistrates or their audit. But perhaps this statement is not entirely correct . . . because about some things the man who made them would not be the only nor the best judge, in the case of professionals whose products come within the knowledge of laymen also; [the ability] to judge a house, for instance, does not belong only to the man who built it but in fact the man who uses the house [that is, the householder] will be an even better judge of it.[94]

Connected to this is yet another problem which served as a subject of polemics between Legalists and Confucians. In Legalist political theory the people were assigned a passive role while action became the preserve of the ruler. Thus the Legalists did not simply consider it unnecessary to initiate the people into the methods and techniques of government, but actually insisted that these arts be kept a closely guarded secret from the close associates of the ruler as well as from the people. The statesman and thinker Shen Pu-hai, prime minister of Han in 351–337 B.C., worked out the techniques of government. Shen Pu-hai said that the ruler who seeks to retain power in his own hands must carefully conceal his views and desires from those around him; otherwise his subordinates will be presented with an opportunity to exploit their knowledge of him and deceive him. Han Fei picked up this idea: "If the ruler conceals his likes and dislikes, he will be able to perceive the true nature of his subordinates."[95] Further developing this theme, Han Fei suggested that the ruler secretly keep an eye on the defects of his subordinates: "Watch but be not watched, listen but be not heard; know but be not known. Cover your tracks and hide your motives, then subordinates will be unable to trace the source of your decisions." [96]

Secrecy, according to Han Fei, is part of the ruler's arsenal, and he employs it to ward off attempts by his close associates to usurp his power. This is attested to by his advice to the ruler. Follow the activity of your subordinates attentively, test them, find and destroy the traitors who wish to pry out the ruler's secret defects; arrest those who were linked to them and deprive them of all support. These measures fit very well into that permanent war which the Legalist ruler must wage against those around him. They are akin to Sun Tzu's advice about how to deceive an enemy. "If you can do something, let the enemy think that you cannot do it; if you are making use of something, let the enemy think that you are not using it." [97]

This approach to government is the direct opposite of the views of the early Confucians. Confucius and Meng Tzu both frequently expressed the thought that the ruler must serve as a model for his people. This in itself excluded the possibility of the ruler engaging in secret actions, for in order to become a model he must be clearly visible to the people. Praising the noble men of antiquity because they openly corrected their own mistakes Meng Tzu says: "These errors were like eclipses of the sun and moon. All the people witnessed them, and when they had reformed them, all the people looked up to them with their former admiration." [98]

Hsün Tzu discusses the question of secrecy in detail. Polemicizing against the Legalists, he says:

> Often today people say: "It is best for a lord to be secretive." This is not so. The lord is the singing-leader of the people; the ruler is the model of the subject. When they hear the singing-leader, they respond: when they see the model they act accordingly. But when the singing-leader is silent, the people are without response; when the model is inaccessible, then the subjects do not act according to it.

Believing that such a situation would threaten to destroy the harmony between the ruler and his subjects, Hsün Tzu says that the conduct of the subjects is directly dependent upon the moral qualities of the rulers:

> When the ruler is upright and sincere, then the subjects are honest and guileless; when the ruler is just and right then the subjects are easily straight. When they are governed well, then they are easily united; when they are honest and guileless, then they are easily employed. When they are easily straight, then they are easily understood. When they are easily united, then the state is strong; when they are easily employed, then the ruler gains glory; when they are easily understood, then the ruler is illustrious. This is the source of good government.
>
> But when the ruler is secretive, then the subjects are confused; when the ruler is inaccessible and difficult to fathom, then the subjects are imbued with falseness; when the ruler is partial and crooked, then the subjects form cliques. When the subjects are confused then they are united with difficulties; when they are imbued with falseness, then they are difficult to employ; when they form cliques, then they are difficult to understand. When they are united with difficulty, then the state is not strong; when they are difficult to employ, then the ruler has no glory; when they are difficult to understand, then the ruler is not illustrious. This is the source of bad government.
>
> Hence it is best for a lord to be open, and not to be hidden. It is best to make things known and not to be secretive. For when the custom (*Tao*) of a lord is to be open, then his subordinates are calm; when the custom (*Tao*) of a lord is to be inaccessible, then his subordinates are uneasy. For when the subjects are calm, then they honour their ruler; when the subordinates are uneasy, then they despise their ruler. For when the ruler is easy to know, then his subjects love their superior; when the ruler is difficult to know, then his subjects fear their ruler. When the subjects love their ruler, the ruler is at rest; when the subjects fear their ruler, the ruler is in danger. Hence there is nothing in his practices (*Tao*) that a lord should hate more than being difficult to know, nothing more dangerous than to cause his subjects to fear him.[99]

The polemic between the early Confucians and the Legalists illumines an important phase of the ideological struggle which was taking place in ancient China. It reveals the profound difference between early Confucianism, which struggled against despotism, and later Confucianism, which became the ideology of a despotic empire.

## The influence of Legalism

The execution of Shang Yang did not lead to the abolition of his reforms. Ch'in, which had become the most powerful state of China through the centralization of power and the establishment of a strong army and disciplined bureaucracy, unified China after defeating the other states in wars that lasted more than a hundred years. Located on the extreme western fringe of China, and viewed as semi-barbaric, Ch'in had almost no aristocracy of its own or cultural traditions, and this undoubtedly assisted its policy of creating a totalitarian state. On returning from a trip to Ch'in, the philosopher Hsün Tzu said that people there feared the officials, while the rites were not observed, music was not performed, and there were no scholars. No wonder that an anticultural doctrine met with little resistance in such a state.

The *Han Fei Tzu* tells us that Shang Yang advised Hsiao Kung, the king of Ch'in, to burn the *Shu Ching* (Book of History) and the *Shih Ching* (Book of Odes).[100] Historians disagree as to whether this actually occurred, but there is no doubt whatsoever that hostility to culture remained the foundation of Legalist teaching. Han Fei repeatedly called for a prohibition of the study of ancient works of literature and philosophy. *Han Fei Tzu* says:

> Therefore, in the state of the enlightened ruler there are no books written on bamboo slips; law supplies the only instruction. There are no sermons on the former kings; the officials serve as the only teachers.[101]

It is well-known that Emperor Ch'in Shih-huang, who unified China, praised *Han Fei Tzu*. This confirms that the burning of books and the execution of scholars in 213 B.C. was by no means provoked only by individual actions of the Confucians against the policies of Ch'in Shih-huang. It was the implementation of the idea of stupefying the people which the proponents of Legalism had been preaching for more than a century.

The indulgence in ferocious reprisals and the destruction of cultural values compromised Legalist theory so fundamentally that in the entire history of Chinese thought no one since has openly dared to proclaim himself a Legalist. Several decades after the Ch'in dynasty was overthrown by a popular uprising, Confucianism was declared the official ideology. But once it had become a doctrine of state, it quickly lost almost all resemblance to the teaching of Confucius and assimilated many elements of Legalist doctrine. Legalism exerted a particularly important influence on the legislation of imperial China. This explains why the legal codes of all Chinese dynasties emphasize penal questions, and why even in matters unrelated to crime we encounter the standard formula, "Anyone who does such and such must be punished in this or that way." Legalism also placed its stamp on the character of the judicial process. Any notion that defense attorneys could participate in the courts was rejected, and the courts proceeded on the basis that the accused was considered guilty until he proved his innocence. Legalist theory was also of assistance in securing the legal approval of torture to extract confessions of guilt. The idea of collective responsibility, which allowed the extermination of all the relatives of "traitors" and "rebels" in full conformity with the law, also derived from the Legalists. The latest research has convincingly demonstrated the need to reexamine the thesis that the government of China was Confucian, a notion that, until recently, has been accepted almost without question.

# CHAPTER FOUR / NATURE AGAINST CIVILIZATION
## Chuang Tzu and Taoism

### The sources of Taoism

Confucianism, Mohism, and Legalism are based on the premise that man is a social being; Confucius could no more conceive of the obedient son outside of the family than he could of the *chün-tzu* outside of his relationship to society. Mo Tzu and the Legalists placed the state first; the representatives of these schools never expressed any doubt that man's place was in society among his fellows, and that with respect to society, man must discharge certain well-defined obligations. But the Taoists entirely rejected this thesis; they looked on society as evil and called on mankind to break loose from society's tenacious embrace, shake off the fetters of false duties and obligations, return to nature, and merge with the unsullied, simple, and genuine life of the universe.

Such views are already encountered in the *Lun yü*, which tells of a meeting between Confucius' disciple Tzu Lu and a hermit.¹ Tzu Lu's description of the hermit's behavior expresses for the first time the most important differences between Confucianism and the approach to social problems which was subsequently taken up by the Taoist philosophers. Tzu Lu says:

> It is not right to refuse to serve one's country. The laws of age and youth may not be set aside. And how can it be right for a man to set aside the duty that binds minister to prince, or in his desire to maintain his own integrity, to subvert the Great Relationship? A *chün-tzu's* service to his country consists in doing such right as

he can. That the Way does not prevail he knows well enough beforehand.[2]

Further, the text cites Confucius' own words. Referring to a number of hermits, he noted, "As for me, I am different from any of these. I have no 'thou shalt' or 'thou shalt not.' " [3] Confucius, who did not share the asocial position of the hermits, decided the question of participation in government on the basis of whether, in the given circumstances, political activity would serve to implement the principles of humanity and justice.

Apparently the term *Tao*, which subsequently characterized this school of ancient Chinese thought, was not yet linked to the views of these hermits. The literal meaning of *Tao* is "road" or "way." But since most ancient times, this concept had been used in a figurative sense with the meaning of "the way of man." *Tao* is often encountered in the *Lun yü* in precisely this meaning. The Taoist philosophers contributed yet another general philosophical meaning to this term—the way which the universe follows—along with that invisible principle which cannot be perceived by the feelings or the intellect, and by virtue of which the universe came into being and developed. The book ascribed to Lao Tzu, the *Tao-te-ching* (Classic of the Way and Its Power) says:

> There was something formless yet complete,
> That existed before heaven and earth;
> Without sound, without substance,
> Dependent on nothing, unchanging,
> All pervading, unfailing.
> One may think of it as the mother of all things under heaven.
> Its true name we do not know;
> Tao is the name that we give it.[4]

The Taoists contrast the principle of *Tao*, which embodies the integrity of the universe, with the vanity of human affairs and aspirations. One who recognizes the insignificance of everything worldly should seek to merge with *Tao* through the aid of mystical enlightenment.

According to tradition, the first Taoist philosopher was Lao Tzu who, Ssu-ma Ch'ien informs us, was an archivist at the Chou court and during a meeting with Confucius set the latter on the path to wisdom. However, by now it has been demonstrated that the Chou archivist who met Confucius and then composed a book of 5,000 characters on his journey to the west is a legendary figure and that the *Tao-te-ching* dates from around 300 B.C. Many scholars now recognize *Chuang Tzu* as the earliest Taoist work, and this prompts us to treat it as the basis of our exposition of ancient Taoist ideas. Another prime consideration is that *Chuang Tzu,* which contains a developed argument as well as parables explaining most of the Taoist theses, is incomparably more suited to analysis of these ideas than the laconic *Tao-te-ching.*

## The life and writings of Chuang Tzu

The short biography of Chuang Tzu which appears in Ssu-ma Ch'ien's *Historical Records* only shows how little was known about his life. He lived ca. 369–286 B.C., and he held some minor post. His revulsion toward the career of a government official is illustrated by an anecdote. The ruler of Ch'u, hearing of Chuang Tzu's talents, offered him the post of prime minister. Chuang Tzu smilingly replied to the king's emissary:

> The position of prime minister is indeed honorable. But have you not had occasion to see a bull which is being prepared for sacrifice? After it is fattened for several years, it is led into the temple and covered with a precious cloth. At that moment it would gladly change places with a neglected piglet, but it's too late. Away with you! I would sooner get pleasure by splashing about in a sewer than allow the ruler to place the yoke on me. I will never become an official; I will preserve the pleasure of following my own inclinations and desires.[5]

Chuang Tzu's organic contempt for political activity as a form of groveling is illustrated by some dialogues from the treatise. Here, for example, is how Chuang Tzu replied to a merchant who, having received 100 chariots from the king of Ch'in was mocking the philosopher's poverty:

> When the king of Ch'in falls ill, he calls for his doctors. The doctor who lances a boil or drains an abscess receives one carriage in payment, but the one who licks his piles for him gets five car-

riages. The lower down the area to be treated, the larger the number of carriages. From the large number of carriages you've got, I take it you must have been treating his piles.[6]

Chuang Tzu's belief in freedom as the highest good and his disdain for material things is reflected in a conversation with the King of Wei. When Chuang Tzu, dressed in coarse linen clothes covered with patches and sandals fastened with rope, walked past the king, the latter asked why he lived in such straitened circumstances. Chuang Tzu replied:

> I am poor, but I am not in distress! When a man possesses the Way and its Virtue but cannot put them into practice, then he is in distress. When his clothes are shabby and his shoes worn through, then he is poor, but he is not in distress.[7]

*Chuang Tzu,* from which these dialogues are taken, is one of the masterpieces of Chinese philosophical prose. A free and unrestrained flight of fantasy distinguishes it from the other treatises containing the teachings of the other schools of ancient Chinese thought. We referred above to the peculiar historicism of the Chinese language and literature which is expressed in a fondness for the concrete, and the elucidation of abstract concepts through the use of historical examples. Chuang Tzu, who called on people to throw off the fetters society had laid upon them, somehow accomplished this liberating breakthrough by his very creativity. In contrast to the short sayings of the *Lun yü,* the sermon-like tone of *Mo Tzu,* and the oppressive narrowmindedness of the *Shang-chün shu,* philosophic ideas are expressed in *Chuang Tzu* through parables and dialogues in which various historical figures participate (for example, Confucius, who voices mostly Taoist sayings), mythical persons, and fantastic beings like Chaos and the Base of Heaven. It is difficult to define the genre of this work; its various fragments are quite diverse and unlike each other. But we shall probably be closest to the truth if we call it a collection of philosophical parables. The first seven chapters are the core, and perhaps derive from the thinker himself. The ideas elaborated in the remaining twenty-six chapters are the work of his pupils and followers. Several of these chapters were written considerably later than the basic text. To this group belongs chapter 33, which presents the first survey of philosophical schools in Chinese literature. Chuang Tzu himself is appraised there in the following terms:

> He expounded [his thoughts] in odd and outlandish terms, in brash and bombastic language, in unbound and unbordered phrases, abandoning himself to the times without partisanship, not looking at things from one angle only. He believed that the world was drowned in turbidness and that it was impossible to address it in sober language. So he used "goblet words" to give a ring of truth, and "imputed words" to impart greater breadth. He came and went alone with the pure spirit of Heaven and earth, yet he did not view the ten thousand things with arrogant eyes. . . . Though his words seem to be at sixes and sevens, yet among the sham and waggery there are things worth observing, for they are crammed with truths that never come to an end.
>
> Above he wandered with the Creator, below he made friends with those who have gotten outside of life and death, who know nothing of beginning or end. As for the Source, his grasp of it was broad, expansive, and penetrating; profound, liberal, and unimpeded. As for the Ancestor, he may be said to have tuned and accommodated himself to it and to have risen on it to the greatest heights. Nevertheless, in responding to change and expounding on the world of things, he set forth principles that will never cease to be valid, an approach that can never be shuffled off.[8]

Lest our praise of this work appear to be unsubstantiated, let us cite a passage that may give some idea of the style.

> Master Sang-hu, Meng-tzu Fan, and Master Ch'in-chang, three friends, said to each other, "who can join with others without joining with others? Who can do with others without doing with others? Who can climb up to heaven and wander in the mists, roam the infinite, and forget life forever and forever?" The three men looked at each other and smiled. There was no disagreement in their hearts and so they became friends.
>
> After some time had passed without event, Master Sang-hu died. He had not yet been buried when Confucius, hearing of his death, sent Tzu-kung to assist at the funeral. When Tzu-kung arrived, he found one of the dead man's friends weaving frames for silk-worms, while the other strummed a lute. Joining their voices, they sang this song:

Ah, Sang-hu!
Ah, Sang-hu!
You have gone back to your true form
While we remain as men, O!

Tzu-kung hastened forward and said, "May I be so bold as to ask what sort of ceremony is this—singing in the very presence of the corpse?"

The two men looked at each other and laughed. "What does this man know of the meaning of ceremony?" they said.

Tzu-kung returned and reported to Confucius what had happened. "What sort of men are they anyway?" he asked. "They pay no attention to proper behavior, disregard their personal appearance and, without so much as changing the expression on their faces, sing in the very presence of the corpse! I can think of no name for them! What sort of men are they?"

"Such men as they," said Confucius, "wander beyond the realm; men like me wander within it. Beyond and within can never meet. It was stupid of me to send you to offer condolences. Even now they have joined with the Creator as men to wander in the single breath of heaven and earth. They look upon life as a swelling tumor, a protruding wen, and upon death as the draining of a sore or the bursting of a boil. To men such as these, how could there be any question of putting life first or death last? . . . They forget liver and gall, cast aside ears and eyes, turning and revolving, ending and beginning again, unaware of where they start or finish. Idly they roam beyond the dust and dirt; they wander free and easy in the service of inaction. Why should they fret and fuss about the ceremonies of the vulgar world and make a display for the ears and eyes of the common herd?" [9]

## Human individuality

In this passage we become acquainted with people who challenge generally accepted rules of propriety. The refusal to submit to social conventions, and the perception of them as unessential, unnecessary, and pitiful, implies that man has within himself something he can counterpose to society. Confucius is made to express the thought that such people can wander on the far side of the dust and dirt of the world without fearing death. The idea of man setting himself up against society and rejecting it is one of Chuang Tzu's basic themes.

Following the deep-rooted tradition of ascribing everything good to far distant times, Chuang Tzu likewise says that in
antiquity there were genuine men who neither feared loneliness,
performed heroic feats, nor schemed. Therefore, when things
went awry they had no need to feel sorry; when things went well
they had nothing to take pride in. That they had been born gave
them no joy; that they must die caused them no sorrow. They
looked on everything with calm indifference, they "did not use
their minds to repel *Tao* from their understanding, and they did
not think they could assist Heaven by the fact that they were
people." [10] Such people had stout hearts and calm features. Their
coldness was that of autumn; their warmth that of spring. And all
their feelings were like the four seasons of the year. In their
closeness to nature, they became like *Tao,* and thus acquired
supernatural powers. They could pass through water without
getting wet, and through fire without getting burned.

Thus to the falsity of society the perfect man (*sheng jen*)
counterposes a merging with nature. The contrast between the
true and beautiful world of nature and the rotten, artificial, and
false world of society runs through all the chapters of *Chuang
Tzu.* Here, for example, is how it appears in a dialogue between
the ancient rulers Yao and Shun. Shun asks Yao what is on his
mind. Yao replies that he neither exalts himself before the pow-
erless nor turns away the poor; he grieves over the dying, re-
joices over the newborn, and takes pity on widows. Such an answer in no way satisfies Shun. "Shun said, 'Admirable, as far as
admirableness goes. But not yet great.' " And he explains what
he means:

> "Heaven raised on high, earth in peace, sun and moon shining,
> the four seasons marching—if you could be like the constant suc-
> cession of day and night, the clouds which move, the rains that
> fall!" Hearing this Yao exclaimed, "You are one who joins with
> Heaven; I am one who joins with man." [11]

This same theme is developed in a conversation between
Confucius and Lao Tan, who appears in *Chuang Tzu* as a messen-
ger of Taoist truths. A number of contemporary scholars, follow-

ing Ssu-ma Ch'ien, identify him with Lao Tzu. When Confucius began to expound the Classics to Lao Tan, the latter interrupted him with the words:

> "This will take forever! Just let me hear the gist of the thing!"
>
> "The gist of it," said Confucius, "is humanity and justice."
>
> "May I ask if humanity and justice belong to the inborn nature of man?" said Lao Tan.
>
> "Of course," said Confucius. "If the *chün-tzu* lacks humanity, he will get nowhere; if he lacks justice, he cannot even stay alive. Humanity and justice are truly the inborn nature of man. What else could they be?"
>
> Lao Tan said, "May I ask your definition of humanity and justice?"
>
> Confucius said, "To be glad and joyful in mind; to embrace universal love and be without partisanship—this is the true form of humanity and justice."
>
> Lao Tan said, "Hmmm—close—except for the last part. 'Universal love'—that's a rather nebulous ideal, isn't it? And to be without partisanship is already a kind of partisanship. Do you want the world to keep from losing its simplicity? Heaven and earth hold fast to their constant ways, the sun and moon to their brightness, the stars and planets to their ranks, the birds and beasts to their flocks, the trees and shrubs to their stands." [12]

The contrast between man and nature is made most often in *Chuang Tzu* by counterposing man to the animals. They are precisely the connecting link between man and *Tao;* on the one hand they are close to man, and on the other they merge with universal life and lack that consciousness which the Taoists hate. In one instance Lao Tan cites for Confucius the example of the snow goose "who needs no daily bath to stay white," and the crow who "needs no daily inking to stay black." The simplicity of their whiteness and blackness transcends the vanity of human words and actions. [13]

According to Chuang Tzu, merging with nature means forgetting about men. This is conveyed through the image of the fish who press upon each other for moisture when the streams and rivers are drying up. But when there is enough water in the rivers, the fish forget each other and swim their separate ways. One should aspire toward this mutual oblivion (*hsiang wang*).

Chuang Tzu places the following words in the mouth of Confucius:

> Fish thrive in water, man thrives in the Way. For those that thrive in water, dig a pond and they will find nourishment enough. For those that thrive in the Way, don't bother about them and their lives will be secure. So it is said, the fish forget each other in the rivers and lakes, and men forget each other in the arts of the Way.[14]

The path toward such oblivion is marked out in a speech by Confucius who, in this passage of *Chuang Tzu,* is assigned the role of a Taoist preacher. Confucius dissuades Yen Hui from aiding the inhabitants of a suffering kingdom. Rejecting all of Yen Hui's plans, Confucius advises him to keep a fast—not an ordinary fast, however, but a fast of consciousness. This means that he must liberate his consciousness from all external impressions so that *Tao* may fill the emptiness. Then, he will be distant from people even when among them. Without moving from his place he can gallop through distant countries; wise without knowledge, he will begin to fly without wings. Yen Hui reacts to these recommendations with an important question: "Before I heard this, I was certain that I was Hui. But now that I have heard it, there is no more Hui. Can this be called emptiness?" [15] Confucius' positive response to Yen Hui's question shows that the conscious goal of the Taoist preachers was a rebirth of the initiate. As a result of his liberation from all ties with the world of man he would feel himself to be an entirely new person, having nothing in common with his pre-enlightenment self.

Progress along this path is described in another conversation between Confucius and Yen Hui.

> Yen Hui said, "I'm improving!"
>     Confucius said, "What do you mean by that?"
>     "I've forgotten humanity and justice!"
>     "That's good. But you still haven't got it."
>     Another day, the two met again and Yen Hui said, "I'm improving!"
>     "What do you mean by that?"
>     "I've forgotten rites and music!"
>     "That's good. But you still haven't got it."

After another day Yen Hui again says that he has improved and explains that he can sit down and forget everything. When Confucius asks what this means Yen Hui replies, "I smash up my limbs and body, drive out perception and intellect, cast off form, do away with understanding, and make myself identical with the Great Thoroughfare." [16]

Such is the image of the Taoist sage (*sheng jen*) which emerges from the pages of *Chuang Tzu*. In contrast to the *chün-tzu*—the ideal man—the *sheng jen* is more nearly a superman. In his identification with *Tao* he sheds all human qualities, severs all his ties, and emerges on the other side of good and evil. The frame of human existence and the norms of morality, as well as all other norms, no longer apply to him. Acting like a force of nature, he performs good deeds or destroys whole kingdoms with equal indifference.

There is yet another side to the question. In counterposing nature to society, the Taoists rejected the latter's right to control people's lives. Confucius spoke of the value of the *chün-tzu*, and said that a gentleman could not become the instrument of another's will. One who harmoniously combines high culture, intellect, a feeling of responsibility, and consciousness of moral duty can with full justice be called a person. According to I. S. Kon's definition, the concept of personality

> denotes a specific individual . . . as a subject of action, in the unity of his individual characteristics . . . and his social roles. . . . On the other hand, personality is understood as the social quality of an individual, as the integrated aggregate of socially significant features which have been formed in the process of direct and indirect interaction of the given person with other persons and which make of him a subject of labor, of knowledge and of social intercourse.[17]

Taoist teaching, which rejects the notion of man as a social being, clearly has no room for the category of human personality. But the Taoists insisted that man as a biological entity cannot be sacrificed to any considerations of political utility, expedience, or social interest. His life belongs to him and him alone; it is his unique and sacred property. In this sense one may discern a certain coincidence of views between the early Confucians and the Taoists. Both of them viewed man as an end, not a means. In this they presented a united front against the Mohist-Legalist exaltation of organization and the state machine and the lowering of man to the role of an insignificant detail. To be sure there is a difference. The Confucians' stress on the inherent value of the *chün-tzu*, that is, human personality, points to a certain aristocratism which contrasts with the democratic inclinations of the Taoists who spoke of the value of each human individuality. In contrast to personality, "individuality as the uniqueness of each separate person is a biological fact above all." [18]

In many parables, *Chuang Tzu* asserts the notion of the value of every being, and the lawfulness of his claim to live his life to its natural conclusion without having it cut off in mid-path. For example, Chuang Tzu tells about a carpenter who saw an enormous oak—one of the local wonders—standing in his path, and walked right past it without so much as a glance. To his pupil who wondered at this display of indifference, the carpenter said:

> "Forget it—say no more! It's a worthless tree! Make boats out of it and they'd sink; make coffins and they'd rot in no time; make vessels and they'd break at once. . . . there's nothing it can be used for. That's how it got to be so old!"
>
> After Carpenter Shih had returned home, the oak tree appeared to him in a dream and said, "What are you comparing me with? Are you comparing me with the cultivated trees? . . . as soon as their fruit is ripe, they are torn apart and subjected to abuse. . . . Their utility makes life miserable for them, and they don't get to finish out the years Heaven gave to them, but they are cut off in mid-journey. They bring it on themselves—the pulling and tearing of the common mob. And it's the same with all other things.
>
> "As for me, I've been trying for a long time to be of no use, . . . This is of great use to me. If I had been of some use, would I ever have grown this large?" [19]

This same idea is expressed in three more parables. One of them, similar to the preceding one, tells of an enormous tree with such twisted and knotty branches that it could not be used as material for anything. It had attained its great size because of this. The next parable tells of "the unhappiness of being material." People cut down trees for many reasons; therefore none of them can complete their lives but fall in mid-growth. The last parable speaks of men, not of trees. Its hero is the hunchback Shu who was not drafted for the army or for compulsory labor, but who received produce when it was distributed among invalids and the sick. All these parables end with the following sentence. "All men know the use of the useful, but nobody knows the use of the useless." [20]

Henri Maspero has shown that one of the sources of Taoism was a quest for longevity and even immortality.[21] The Taoists and their predecessors tried to achieve this by abandoning society and hiding out as hermits. This may explain why the lives of the founders of Taoism are so little known. Wolfgang Bauer noted a paradoxical fact which is connected to the attention paid to individual life and the anxiety about preserving it. It is in the Taoist sources, which call for the personality to dissolve itself within the universal whole, that first-person experiences appear for the first time in Chinese literature.[22] In Confucian treatises the author usually speaks of himself in the third person, often hiding behind the formula "they say . . ."; but in a number of the sayings of the Taoist founders the philosopher steps forth in his own name, without trying to drape himself in someone else's authority. Chapter 20 of the *Tao-te-ching* may serve as an example of this. In it the hermit says bitterly:

> All men, indeed, are wreathed in smiles,
> As though feasting after the Great Sacrifice,
> As though going up to the Spring Carnival.
> I alone am inert, like a child that has not yet given sign,
> Like an infant that has not yet smiled.
> I droop and drift, as though I belonged nowhere.
> All men have enough and to spare;
> I alone seem to have lost everything.
> Mine is indeed the mind of a very idiot,
> So dull am I.
> The world is full of people that shine;
> I alone am dark.

They look lively and self-assured;
I alone, depressed.
I seem unsettled as the ocean;
Blown adrift, never brought to a stop.[23]

That such a passage could appear in a Taoist treatise shows that Taoism, with its sense of exclusivity and the uniqueness of the individual existence, allowed the expression of sentiments that could not fit into the framework of familial and sociopolitical relations.

## The condemnation of civilization

The passages already cited demonstrate the polemical tone of *Chuang Tzu*. Its summons to leave the world of man and merge with the world of nature is inseparably linked with a trenchant critique of civilization, a critique directed against the morality and culture of Chuang Tzu's own society as well as against human activity in general.

Proclaiming ethics as a superficial and unnatural growth akin to a sixth finger or a membrane between the toes, Chuang Tzu says: "He who is fork-fingered with humanity will tear out the Virtue given him and stifle his inborn nature in order to seize fame and reputation." [24]

Ethical norms are likened to a procrustean bed used to amputate the legs of cranes or stretch the legs of ducks. Chuang Tzu compares them to a carpenter's tools which destroy the nature of wood. This last reproach evokes the craftsmen's model from which the Legalists derived their approach to government. It is noteworthy that the same comparison figures in the Confucian treatise, *Meng Tzu*. However, Meng Tzu vigorously rejects the comparison which his interlocutor offers between the process of fashioning a cup out of willow, and that of creating humanity and justice from human nature.

> Can you, leaving untouched the nature of the willow, make with it cups and bowls? You must do violence and injury to the willow, before you can make cups and bowls with it. If you must do violence and injury to the willow in order to make cups and bowls with it, on

your principles you must in the same way do violence and injury to mankind in order to fashion from it humanity and justice! Your words, alas! would certainly lead all men on to reckon humanity and justice to be calamities.[25]

Thus, the early Confucian philosophers asserted that humanity and justice can be attained only through humane means. But the problem that arises here of the relationship between ends and means could never appear within Taoist theory, which in general rejects any action whatsoever.

However, the most persistent attack on ethics is conducted from a different position. Chuang Tzu frequently repeats his assertion that ethical norms are dangerous, above all, to those who adhere to them. He harshly condemns those who unnaturally expose themselves to such danger without cause. It is interesting that while objecting to Confucius' ideal from this perspective, Chuang Tzu attempted to identify the *chün-tzu* with the perfect Taoist man. He does not consider a *chün-tzu* just any person who pays no attention to profit or danger. Citing a long list of people who were famous for their self-sacrifice, he says, "all of them slaved in the service of other men, took joy in bringing other men joy, but could find no joy in any joy of their own." [26]

Thus, while in relation to *Tao*, the great law of the universe, the Taoists view life and death as matters of indifference and think there is no reason to mourn the deceased, in relation to society they believe that the preservation of one's nature, that is, one's self-preservation, is the highest value and the greatest obligation. Self-preservation is possible only by refraining from all activity, and therefore inaction (*wu wei*) is proclaimed as the greatest virtue. Only he who values his own life more than all-under-Heaven and who therefore practices inaction may be trusted with the governing of all-under-Heaven. Such a person, passionless and indifferent, will allow all things to follow their natural course.[27]

Since the chief goal is self-preservation, the difference between good and evil, tyrants and benefactors disappears and all moral judgements become unimportant. Such is the sense of a number of Chuang Tzu's parables. For example:

The slave boy and the slave girl were out together herding their sheep, and both of them lost their flocks. Ask the slave boy how it happened: well, he had a bundle of writing slips and was reading a book. Ask the slave girl how it happened: well, she was playing a game of toss-and-wait-your-turn. They went about the business in different ways, but in losing their sheep they were equal. Po Yi died for reputation at the foot of Shou-Yang mountain; Robber Chih died for gain on top of Eastern Mound. The two of them died different deaths, but in destroying their lives and blighting their inborn nature they were equal. Why then must we say that Po Yi was right and Robber Chih was wrong?

Everyone in the world risks his life for something. If he risks it for humanity and justice, then custom names him a gentleman (*chün-tzu*) if he risks it for goods and wealth then custom names him a petty man (*hsiao jen*). The risking is the same. . . . How then can we pick out the gentleman from the petty man in such a case? [28]

According to Chuang Tzu's theory, any inspiration or activity, whether it is inspired by low or by lofty goals, is undeserving of approbation unless it is directed at self-preservation. Chuang Tzu proclaims that whether activity is moral or amoral makes no difference whatsoever, but in fact he attacks the principles of morality with particular bitterness, as if sensing that they pose the most serious threat to his doctrine. An example of this ferocious attack is the passage dealing with the question of whether a robber has his own morality (Way). The Robber Chih says:

How could he get anywhere if he didn't have a Way? Making shrewd guesses as to how much booty is stashed away in the room is sageliness; being the first one in is bravery; being the last one out is righteousness; knowing whether the job can be pulled off or not is wisdom; dividing the loot up fairly is humanity. No one in the world ever succeeded in becoming a great thief if he didn't have all five! [29]

The characteristics of the gentleman (*chün-tzu*) are degraded to the level of traits essential to the success of a base activity.

In Chuang Tzu's eyes, culture is the embodiment of artificiality and the direct antithesis of natural simplicity. In the treatise he unleashes upon it an attack no less fierce than that directed at morality. Comparing culture (like morality) to an unnecessary growth on the body, Chuang Tzu says that extraordinary subtlety of vision leads to a chaotic perception of natural colors, with the result that the eyes become blinded by the glitter of colors and lines. Extraordinary subtlety of hearing hinders the perception of natural sounds and leads to the unnecessary exaltation of music. Superfluous quarrels give rise to the piling up of evidence like tiles on a roof, and people sink down in verbal tricks.[30] Citing the debates between the adherents of Mo Tzu and those of Confucius as an example of meaningless quarrels, Chuang Tzu declares that words can express only a small fraction of *Tao*. Therefore, they are all equally vain, insignificant, and harmful because they distract people from contemplation of the great unity of *Tao*.[31] Contradictory statements mislead people into senseless philosophizing. The second chapter of the *Tao-te-ching* proclaims that:

> When the people of the world all know beauty as beauty
> There arises the recognition of ugliness
> When they all know the good as good
> There arises the recognition of evil. Therefore:
> Being and non-being produce each other
> Difficult and easy complete each other; long and short contrast
> With each other. . . . Front and behind accompany each other
> Therefore the sage manages affairs without action and
> Speaks doctrines without words.[32]

If the truth cannot be expressed in words, it is even more impossible to approach it through bookish learning.

> But books are nothing more than words. Words have value; what is of value in words is meaning. Meaning has something it is pursuing, but the thing that it is pursuing cannot be put into words and handed down. The world values words and hands down books but, though the world values them, I do not think them worth valuing. What the world takes to be value is not real value.
>
> What you can look at and see are forms and colors; what you can listen to and hear are names and sounds. What a pity!— that the men of the world should suppose that form and color, name and sound are sufficient to convey the truth of a thing. It is because in the end they are not sufficient that "those who know

do not speak, those who speak do not know." But how can the world understand this!

Duke Huan was in the hall reading a book. The wheelwright P'ien, who was in the yard below chiseling a wheel, laid down his mallet and chisel, stepped up into the hall, and said to Duke Huan, "This book Your Grace is reading—may I venture to ask whose words are in it?"

"The words of the sages," said the duke.

"Are the sages still alive?"

"Dead long ago," said the duke.

"In that case, what you are reading there is nothing but the chaff and dregs of the men of old!"

"Since when does a wheelwright have permission to comment on the books I read?" said Duke Huan. "If you have some explanation, well and good. If not it's your life!"

Wheelwright P'ien said, "I look at it from the point of view of my own work. . . . You can't put it into words, and yet there's a knack to it somehow. I can't teach it to my son and he can't learn it from me. So I've gone along for seventy years and at my age I'm still chiseling wheels.

"When the men of old died, they took with them the things that couldn't be handed down. So what you are reading there must be nothing but the chaff and dregs of the men of old." [33]

Rebelling against any sort of refinement, subtlety or sophistication, Chuang Tzu also opposed technical innovations and labor-saving devices. He saw in them, as he saw in erudition, a departure from natural simplicity and plainness. *Chuang Tzu* contains the following anecdote on this theme. Confucius' pupil Tzu Kung saw, during his travels, a man working in his garden. Having excavated an irrigation ditch, he was filling it with water which he drew from a well in a big pitcher. Noticing that the gardener had achieved pitiable results despite his great efforts, Tzu Kung said to him: "There is a machine for this sort of thing. In one day it can water a hundred fields, demanding very little effort and producing excellent results. Wouldn't you like one?" When Tzu Kung explained how the well sweep was constructed, the gardener, anger flushing his face, said:

"I've heard my teacher say, where there are machines, there are bound to be machine worries; where there are machine worries, there are bound to be machine hearts. With a machine heart in your breast, you've spoiled what was pure and simple, and without the pure and simple, the life of the spirit knows no rest. Where the life of the spirit knows no rest, *Tao* will cease to buoy you up. It's not that I don't know about your machine—I would be ashamed to use it!" [34]

This response from the gardener, we are told, discomfited Tzu Kung so much that he did not recover his composure till he had gone thirty *li* (about ten miles). To his pupils, who asked why he was so upset, he said:

I used to think there was only one real man in the world. I didn't know there was this other one. I have heard Confucius say that in affairs you aim for what is right, and in undertakings you aim for success. To spend little effort and achieve big results—that is the Way of the sage. Now it seems that this isn't so. He who holds fast to *Tao* is complete in Virtue; being complete in Virtue, he is complete in body; being complete in body, he is complete in spirit; and to be complete in spirit is the Way of the sage. He is content to live among the people, to walk by their side, and never know where he is going. . . . Achievement, profit, machines, skill—they have no place in this man's mind! . . . He may be called a man of Complete Virtue. I—I am a man of the wind-blown waves. [35]

Censuring any activity connected with morality and culture as a "departure from nature," Chuang Tzu saw contemporary government as the leading example of harmful human activity. With striking forcefulness, he described the consequences of this activity.

Lao Tan, the mouthpiece for Chuang Tzu's ideas, trying to convince people "not to touch the human heart," says:

In ancient times the Yellow Emperor first used humanity and justice to meddle with the minds of men. Yao and Shun followed him and worked till there was no more down on their thighs, no more hair on their shins, trying to nourish the bodies of the men of the world. They grieved their five vital organs in the practice of humanity and justice, taxed their blood and breath in the establishment of laws and standards. But still some men would not submit to their rule, and so they had to exile Huan Tou to Mount Ch'ung, drive away the San-miao tribes to the region of San-wei, and banish Kung to the Dark City. This shows that they could not make the world submit.

By the time the kings of the Three Dynasties appeared, the world was in great consternation indeed. On the lowest level there were men like the tyrant Chieh and the Robber Chih, on the highest, men like Tseng and Shih, and the Confucianists and Mo-ists rose up all around. Then joy and anger eyed each other with suspicion, stupidity and wisdom duped each other, good and bad called each other names, falsehood and truth slandered one another, and the world sank into a decline. There was no more unity to the Great Virtue, and the inborn nature and fate shattered and fell apart. The world coveted knowledge and the hundred clans were thrown into turmoil. Then there were axes and saws to shape things, ink and plumb lines to trim them, mallets and gouges to poke holes in them, and the world, muddled and deranged was in great confusion. The crime lay in this meddling with men's minds. So it was that worthy men crouched in hiding below the great mountains and yawning cliffs, and the lords of the ten thousand chariots fretted and trembled above in their ancestral halls.

In the world today, the victims of the death penalty lie heaped together, the bearers of the cangue tread on each other's heels, the sufferers of punishments are never out of each other's sight. And now come the Confucianists and the Mo-ists, waving their arms, striding into the very midst of the fettered and manacled men. Ah, that they should go this far, that they should be so brazen, so lacking in any sense of shame! Who can convince me that sagely wisdom is not in fact the wedge that fastens the cangue, humanity and justice are not in fact the loop and lock of these fetters and manacles? How do I know that Tseng and Shih are not the whistling arrows that signal the approach of Chieh and Chih? Therefore, I say, cut off sageness, cast away wisdom, and the world will be in perfect order.[36]

To the false, artificial civilization hobbled by thousands of conventions, Chuang Tzu counterposes the simple, pure, and free world of nature. He sees the ideal of nature in the image of wild horses.

Horses' hoofs are made for treading frost and snow, their coats for keeping out wind and cold. To munch grass, drink from the stream, lift up their feet and gallop—this is the true nature of horses. Though they might possess great terraces and fine halls, they would have no use for them! [37]

In ancient times, men too approached a state of simple desire. They had not yet tasted culture and were satisfied with the bare minimum. Chuang Tzu describes this golden age as follows:

> The people have their constant inborn nature. To weave for their clothing, to till for their food—this is the Virtue they share. . . . Therefore in a time of Perfect Virtue the gait of men is slow and ambling; their gaze is steady and mild. In such an age mountains have no paths or trails, lakes no boats or bridges. The ten thousand things live species by species, one group settled close to another. . . . In this age of Perfect Virtue men live the same as birds and beasts, group themselves side by side with the ten thousand things. Who then knows anything about "gentleman" or "petty man"? Dull and unwitting, men have no wisdom; thus their Virtue does not depart from them. Dull and unwitting, they have no desire; this is called uncarved simplicity.[38]

In those days people were happy with plain food, were content with their clothing and found solace in their dwellings. They did not leave their villages even though they reached a ripe old age. The kingdoms were so small then, that you could see from one to the other, and the inhabitants of one kingdom could hear the crowing of roosters and the barking of dogs from the other.[39]

The counterposing of the "natural" savage to "unnatural" civilized man is a theme encountered in the social thought of ancient Greece and modern Europe as well. Noting that several Enlightenment thinkers, as well as Tolstoy in a later period, make this contrast between the "natural" and the "unnatural," Yu. M. Lotman writes that from this point of view "what is true and valuable are the direct realities: man in his anthropological essence, physical happiness, labor, food, life perceived as a definite biological process." In this perspective symbols and especially words become a synonym for lies. The highest criterion of value is sincerity, which is contrasted to words; "the bearer of truth is not only the infant, or the savage outside of society, but also the animal who is outside of language." [40]

This is an apt description of Chuang Tzu's world view—

one that, curiously, the ancient Greek Cynics also defended. The very name of this school (*kinos* means dog in ancient Greek) is connected with the call to become like the animals. Diogenes, the most famous of the Cynics, tried to implement this call. He believed that to live in accordance with nature meant to reject all excesses of culture and implied an ability to survive on a bare minimum. Declaring that culture was a form of violence against the human being, Diogenes rejected morality and the state and demanded that man return to his primal or even to the animal state.[41]

Another interesting comparison is between Chuang Tzu's ideas and those of Rousseau. Like Chuang Tzu, Rousseau directed a devastating critique against civilization and contrasted it to the life of savages. He wrote:

> So long as men remained content with their rustic huts, so long as they were satisfied with clothes made of the skins of animals and sewn together with thorns and fishbones, adorned themselves only with feathers and shells, and continued to paint their bodies different colours, to improve and beautify their bows and arrows, and to make sharp-edged stone fishing boats or clumsy musical instruments; in a word, so long as they undertook only what a single person could accomplish . . . they lived free, healthy, honest and happy lives, so long as their nature allowed. . . . But from the moment one man began to stand in need of the help of another; from the moment it appeared advantageous to any one man to have enough provisions for two, equality disappeared, property was introduced, work became indispensable, and vast forests became smiling fields, which man had to water with the sweat of his brow, and where slavery and misery were soon to germinate and grow up with the crops.[42]

Arguing that sciences and art, which breed egoism and indifference to the sufferings of others, exert a particularly harmful influence on man, Rousseau refers approvingly in his first Treatise to the Sultan Achmet's prohibition of printing, and to the burning of the Alexandria library.

However, although Rousseau and Chuang Tzu are united by their exaltation of savagery to the detriment of civilization, Rousseau lacks any trace of Chuang Tzu's amoralism. On the contrary, Rousseau condemns man's civilization on moral grounds. In his opinion, science, art, and the artful designs of social and political hierarchies force man to forget his true nature, which consists of a natural revulsion at the sufferings of his fellow creatures. While Chuang Tzu persuades people to adopt an attitude of calm indifference, and says that although the perfect man has a human form he lacks human emotions, Rousseau appears as a defender of feeling against the encroachments of reason. Rousseau's protest against inequality and social injustice is predicated on a belief in man's deep interest in a just social order, but for Chuang Tzu any society is doomed because it has departed from natural simplicity. Rousseau ascribed enormous importance to education; Chuang Tzu disbelieved entirely in the possibility of education. For Rousseau the decline of the golden age began with the appearance of private property. He writes:

> The first man who, having enclosed a piece of ground, bethought himself of saying "This is mine," and found people simple enough to believe him, was the real founder of civil society. From how many crimes, wars, murders, from how many horrors and misfortunes might not any one have saved mankind, by pulling up the stakes or filling up the ditch, and crying to his fellows: "Beware of listening to this impostor; you are undone if you once forget that the fruits of the earth belong to us all, and the earth itself to nobody." [43]

In contrast, Chuang Tzu considers knowledge to be the root of evil. "So the world is dulled and darkened by great confusion. The blame lies in this coveting of knowledge." [44]

Now let us turn our attention to a particular aspect of Chuang Tzu. In addition to his call to desert civilization (which he saw as hopelessly bad) for a mystical merging with *Tao* (this might be accompanied by a literal flight into the "desert" or "the caves of great mountains"), Chuang Tzu points out one other path—the destruction of civilization. The theory of its primordial worthlessness created an ideological basis for such a possibility.

> Cut off sageliness, cast away wisdom, and then the great thieves will cease. Break the jades, crush the pearls, and petty thieves will no longer rise up. Burn the tallies, shatter the seals, and the peo-

ple will be simple and guileless. Hack up the bushels, snap the balances in two, and the people will no longer wrangle. Destroy and wipe out the laws that the sage has made for the world, and at last you will find you can reason with the people.

Discard and confuse the six tones, smash and unstring the pipes and lutes, stop up the ears of the blind musician K'uang, and for the first time the people of the world will be able to hold on to their hearing. Wipe out patterns and designs, scatter the five colors, glue up the eyes of Li Chu, and for the first time the people of the world will be able to hold on to their eyesight. Destroy and cut to pieces the curve and plumb line, throw away the compass and square, shackle the fingers of the Artisan Ch'ui, and for the first time the people of the world will possess real skill. Thus it is said, "Great skill is like clumsiness." Put a stop to the ways of Tseng and Shih, gag the mouths of Yang and Mo, wipe out and reject humanity and righteousness, and for the first time the Virtue of the world will reach the state of Mysterious Leveling. . . . When men hold on to their wisdom, the world will no longer be confused. When men hold on to their Virtue, the world will no longer go awry.[45]

As everyone knows, Rousseau's ideas played a great role in the period in which the French Revolution was prepared and carried out. These ideas received the force of law through the Declaration of the Rights of Man and Citizen and other enactments of the French Revolution. The tendency of Taoist doctrine to encourage the destruction of civilization explains how a teaching that most sinologists look on as a form of peaceful and inoffensive quietism could become the banner of revolt against the existing order.

\* \* \*

The fate of Taoism through the centuries is filled with surprising contrasts. This doctrine, which so adamantly stressed indifference to the vanities of life and preached calm acceptance of death, served in the second century A.D. as the basis of a religion whose goal was a method of achieving longevity and immortality. During this period Buddhism penetrated China. On the model of the Buddhist religious organization, a Taoist church was created with numerous temples and monasteries, and a

Taoist classical canon (*Tao tsang*), numbering more than a thousand works, was compiled. One of the founders of the Taoist religion was Chang Ling who became famous because he taught how to achieve longevity and compounded an elixir of immortality. In the latter half of the second century A.D., in the western province of Szechwan, he founded a sect each of whose initiates had to contribute five pecks of rice (hence its name—"Teaching of the Five Pecks of Rice"). The followers of Chang Ling called him the "Heavenly Teacher," and after a time this became an official title which was handed down to his successors. They considered themselves the heads of the Taoist church, but actually they enjoyed no particular authority among the majority of Taoist priests.

The revolutionary potential of Taoism as a peasant utopia was expressed in the teachings of another Taoist sect, founded in the eastern part of China by Chang Chüeh, a contemporary of Chang Ling. "The Way of the Great Peace" which this sect followed proclaimed that after the overthrow of the Han dynasty, a new kingdom of universal peace, happiness, and equality would be instituted. The followers of Chang Chüeh did not limit themselves to promises. They established village communes in which they tried to implement the principles of equality, and created a powerful military organization which tried to seize power through a lightning blow on the first day of 184 A.D. This attempt failed, and the uprising (called the "Yellow Turban Rebellion") was drowned in blood after a short period.

Subsequently, the most widespread school of Taoism had a doctrine which was radically different from the views of Lao Tzu and Chuang Tzu despite the fact that Lao Tzu became one of the chief Taoist divinities. This new doctrine was propounded by Ko Hung (253–333 A.D.), the author of the treatise *Pao-p'u-tzu* (The Master Who Embraces Simplicity), who combined Taoist magic and occultism with Confucian ethics. Severely censuring Chuang Tzu for his indifference to life and death, Ko Hung said that man can achieve immortality by adhering to a particular diet and way of life. Stressing the importance of nutrition, Ko Hung argued that compounds containing gold and mercury should be the basis of the diet of one aspiring to immortality. The Taoists worked out many other ways of "achieving immortality." Some of them were based on the premise that the main cause of aging was the utilization of the sense organs which were orifices through which the life force slipped away. In order to prevent this, the Taoists recommended stopping up the ears and not exerting the eyes. There were also prescriptions relating to sexual hygiene and methods of correct breathing.

Rejecting the amoralism of Chuang Tzu, Ko Hung advanced an original "theory of merits," according to which observance of the above prescriptions was not enough to attain longevity; good deeds were also necessary. Every good deed was rewarded with the prolongation of life by from three to three hundred days. The term of life was shortened as punishment for evil deeds. Ko Hung wrote that those who wish to become immortal must look on loyalty, filial piety, sincerity, and love of man as the basic rules of conduct. In the course of time, the Taoist religion became more and more syncretic and diffuse as it absorbed elements of Confucianism and Buddhism. Finally, it became an aggregate of the most variegated folk beliefs. Among the Taoist gods there were historical personalities, deified professions, ideas, parts of the body, plants, animals, and so forth. The educated elite viewed this religion with contempt.

The influence of Taoist tradition on Chinese culture, however, far exceeds the bounds of religion. As Joseph Needham, the author of a multivolume work on Chinese science, has shown, Taoism as a current of thought promoted the development of proto-scientific knowledge in China. Taoist thinkers, bewitched by nature, renouncing everyday cares and career anxieties, called for concentration on nature's splendor and her multiple permutations. Sooner or later they had to move from observation to experimentation. This transition was expedited by the respect for handicraft labor and the contempt for book learning which Chuang Tzu fostered, and the search for the elixir of immortality, to which the adherents of Taoism began to devote themselves from the first centuries A.D. A large number of well-known Taoists spent a good deal of their time bent over alchemists' cauldrons. Chinese pharmacology, and a significant part of Chinese medicine too, can be traced back to such occupations.

Taoist proto-science was akin to magic. Experimentation was accompanied by incantations. But this feature was present in the first stages of natural investigation not only in China but in Europe as well. The possibility of distinguishing magic from science appears somewhat late in the history of mankind, and in sixteenth-century Europe science was still usually called natural magic. Kepler studied astrology and even Newton was called "the last of the magicians." The differentiation between magic and experimental science came about only when the methodology of repeated experimentation under the same conditions, combined with the verification of results, began to be used to study the regularities of nature. In Europe this did not occur until the seventeenth century. In China science did not arise independently.

Finally, Taoism exerted a tremendous influence on Chinese art, which was indebted to this doctrine for its most brilliant success—landscape painting. At first serving only as a background for portraiture, landscapes later acquired the status of an independent genre in Chinese art, finally eclipsing portraiture. The works of the first Chinese landscape artists from the fourth and fifth centuries A.D. show the influence of the Taoist striving to merge with nature, to experience participation in the great unity of the world of mountains and rivers. The words of Wang Wei (415–443 A.D.) bear witness to this:

> The wind rises from the green forest, and foaming water rushes in the stream. Alas! Such paintings cannot be achieved by the physical movements of the fingers and the hand, but only by the spirit entering into them. This is the nature of painting.[46]

# SUMMARY

In this analysis of the philosophic outlook of four Chinese thinkers of antiquity, attention has been directed mainly toward their attitude to man, the state, and culture. Summarizing, we arrive at the following conclusions.

Three attitudes toward man may be discerned in ancient Chinese thought. For Confucius, the problem of the personality occupies the central position in his meditations on the world. He considers that man has an infinite capacity for perfecting himself; through the continual and profound assimilation of ancient traditions, permeated with moral and cultural values, he may become a model of the domestic virtues, a personality in which moral nobility and a high level of culture are harmoniously blended. The Confucian school of thought uses the term *chün-tzu* to distinguish this ideal character; it was to become the principal ideal in Chinese civilization. To further inculate the principles of humanity and justice in life, the *chün-tzu* should engage in state employment, though this need not entail the blind execution of orders. Whenever the *chün-tzu* becomes convinced that injustice prevails in the state, and that no means within his power exists to combat this, he should give up his position; poverty and a humble place in life are preferable to the degradation of selling his knowledge and abilities to a despot. Confucius regards the *chün-tzu* not as the means to an end but as the purpose of history.

Chuang Tzu, one of the founders of Taoism, holds a totally contrary view. He emphasizes the contradiction between the artificial world of civilization and the world of nature; the crux of his teaching lies in the exposure of civilization, with its morality, culture, state, and attitude toward man. In his view, man—far from being the crowning achievement of nature—is simply a dismal exception to nature, a feeble degenerate who, forgetful of the calm grandeur of nature, has plunged into the vortex of his own senseless affairs. The aim of everyone desirous of returning to nature and to close communion with the mysterious basic force Tao, which has generated and directed its innumerable transformations, is to escape from the civilized world. This escape lies within the power of the wise alone, who, having rejected human society, achieve harmony with nature. Unlike the *chün-tzu*, the Taoist must forget people and their affairs, cares, and sufferings. Man has acquired value solely as a biological individuality, identifiable with nature and thus rising above society which, consequently, has no right to demand any sacrifices from him.

The basis of Mo Tzu's attitude, later to be adopted by Shang Yang and other Legalists, is that the state is the highest value, whereas a man is no more than an insignificant cog in the state-machine. While Confucius and Chuang Tzu hold that man exercises the right of free will over himself and his actions, the watchword of the Mo Tzu school is "man—the instrument." Hence, the sole important aspect of man's personality is the one that allows him to be manipulated; in other words, man's desire for pleasure and dread of suffering should be directed, through a system of rewards and punishments, toward ensuring unquestioning obedience to a ruler's commands. The supporters of this trend did not recognize man as an ideal; the ideal was an omnipotent and omniscient state.

The Taoist view of human civilization determines its negative attitude toward the state. Consequently, the argument concerning the position of the state is between Taoism and the Confucian school on the one hand, and between Taoism and the Mohists and Legalists on the other. Confucius conceives the state as, essentially, one large family; the father is the ruler, the children are his subjects. Subjects should obey their ruler in the same way that children love and honor their parents. At the same time, Confucius and his disciple, Mencius, stress the point that a ruler should not neglect his parental obligations; he must expend love and care on his subjects. Mencius thinks that unless he does this, the ruler will no longer be a father but a tyrant whose subjects can overthrow and destroy him as if he were a robber.

The concept of the state as one great family led Confucius to the conclusion that laws were of no importance. Most important of all was that the country have a good ruler, one who is both able to set an example of virtue and rectitude, and to select advisers who embody the qualities of the *chün-tzu*. As a result of the conflict created between the law and Chinese moral and cultural values, the concept of law as an embodiment of the norms of justice, directed toward ensuring the rights of citizens and protecting them from oppression—a concept that has prevailed in Europe since Greek antiquity—never took shape in China.

Mo Tzu rejects the concept of the state as family in favor of the view that the state is a machine, the component parts of which can be set in motion at the command of the helmsman-ruler. In place of the Confucian idea that the moral qualities of the ruler and of his advisers are the deciding factor, Mo Tzu claims that governing is a trade similar to that of, say, a butcher. He refuses to regard playing a role in government as the fulfillment of a moral duty, and thus introduces into the problem the method of quantitative analysis. Unlike Confucius, who declares that some people are fitted by their moral qualities for every kind of rule while others are not, Mo Tzu introduces a scale of values for those who, by their knowledge and abilities, are fit to direct various administrative units.

This method, which undoubtedly took shape as a result of administrative experience, marked the transition from the city-state to the large kingdom; it constituted Mo Tzu's legacy to Shang Yang, who perfected the law regulating the system of rewards and punishments. Shang Yang declared that this law must constitute the sole means of regulating man's activity, and must replace all moral norms. But while Mo Tzu's efforts to create an ideal machine of state had been characterized by an antipathy to wars of aggression and a desire to aid the people, Shang Yang openly declared that a powerful state-machine was required chiefly for purposes of warfare and to secure domination over everything under the sun. It should be directed, therefore, against the people, since their enfeeblement would contribute to the strengthening of the state. To this end, the Legalists worked out a series of measures; starting with the people's expropriation and the monopolization of all revenues by the state, these measures culminated in the stunting and stupefying of the people, whose efforts had to be concentrated on agriculture and warfare.

The concept of culture in Confucian teaching is inseparably bound up with the idea of morality. Confucius believed that assimilation of the traditions of antiquity contributed to the cultivation of man's noblest qualities, and provided him with a source of self-expression. Hence, familiarity with ancient poetry, music, rules of conduct, and ritual were as essential to the *chün-tzu* as was concern for his fellow men. The flowering of culture and the welfare of the people signified that the government was in capable hands. Prosperity of this kind was always the outcome of a policy of peace, and would be impossible in a state where militant spirit and desire for new conquests reigned.

This exaltation of culture is opposed by Mo Tzu and Shang Yang, as well as by Chuang Tzu. While insisting that the state's efforts should be directed toward the satisfaction of the people's main requirements—food, clothing and housing—Mo Tzu considers culture an unnecessary luxury and a foolish waste of means. Shang Yang goes further still, claiming that culture is not merely useless, but actually harmful to the state. Poetry, music, history, humanity, justice, and sincerity are termed "lice," parasites that can lead only to the ruin of the state.

Shang Yang and other Legalists called for the strongest possible measures to put down these "parasites." It was the standpoint that formed the ideological basis for the persecution of culture and the burning of books in the year 213 B.C.

The motives underlying this repudiation of culture are, in Chuang Tzu's case, diametrically opposite to those of Mo Tzu and Shang Yang. For one thing, Chuang Tzu repudiates culture simply because he discerns in it a manifestation of the social ties that he detests—those enveloping man in a close network of obligations, contracts, and conventions. Since he detects in the attainment of knowledge—in the refinement of intellect, vision, and hearing—the root of all evils, Chuang Tzu emphasizes the contrast between an unnatural, civilized man and a natural savage. Two courses are open to man in order to avoid these evils— either to flee from civilized society or to destroy it. This last tendency in Taoism is responsible for the fact that, throughout China's history, Taoist teaching has often been adopted as the rallying point of revolutionary peasants.

# NOTES

## Preface to the English edition

1. Thomas Berry, review of *The Religious Life of Man* ed. by F. J. Streng, *Philosophy East and West*, Vol. 24, no. 1, p. 109.

2. F. S. Bykov, "Confucius," *Philosophical Encyclopedia* (in Russian), vol. 3, p. 56 (Moscow, 1964).

3. M. L. Titarenko, "Introduction" to a translation of excerpts of the *Lun yü* in *Anthology of World Philosophy* (in Russian) (Moscow, 1969), vol. 1, p. 190.

4. *Ibid.*

5. See P. S. Popov, *The Sayings of Confucius, His Followers and Others* (in Russian) (St. Petersburg, 1910); *The Chinese Philosopher Meng Tzu*, 1904. In 1972–1973 a two-volume collection of texts in ancient Chinese philosophy was published in the USSR, including translations of excerpts from the *Lun yü* and *Meng Tzu*. See *Ancient Chinese Philosophy. A Collection of Texts* eds. V. G. Burov, R. V. Vyatkin and M. L. Titarenko.

6. Yang Hsing-shun, *The Ancient Chinese Philosopher Lao Tzu and His Teaching* (Moscow, 1950), p. 54.

7. *Ibid.*, p. 80.

8. L. D. Pozdneeva, "Introduction," to *Atheists, Materialists and Dialecticians of Ancient China* (Moscow, 1967), p. 8.

9. *Ibid.*, p. 31.

10. "Introduction," to a translation of excerpts from *Mo Tzu* in *Anthology of World Philosophy* (Moscow, 1969), vol. 1, p. 196.

11. A. A. Petrov, "An Outline of Chinese Philosophy," in *China: A Collection of Articles,* eds. V. M. Alekseev, L. I. Duman, A. A. Petrov (Moscow–Leningrad, 1940), p. 259.

12. F. S. Bykov, *The Genesis of Socio-Political and Philosophical Thought in China* (Moscow, 1966), pp. 216–17.

13. E. P. Sinitsyn, "Introduction," to a translation of excerpts from *Han Fei: Ancient Chinese Philosophy* (Moscow, 1973), vol. 2, p. 224.

14. *Ibid.*

15. L. S. Perelomov, *The Book of the Ruler of Shang District,* translation from the Chinese with an introduction and commentary (Moscow, 1968), p. 53. According to Perelomov, the views of Shang Yang reflected the demands of the social elite for the abolition of hereditary posts and for the acceptance of "sons of wealthy families" into the government. This demand coincided with the ruler's desire to sever the rights of the aristocrats.

16. *Ibid.,* pp. 82–83.

17. *Ibid.,* p. 94.

18. V. A. Rubin, "Two Sources of Chinese Political Thought," U.S.S.R. Academy of Sciences, *Social Science Today,* no. 3, 1969. (Originally published in Russian in 1967 in *Voprosy Istorii,* 1967, No. 3, pp. 70–81).

19. See the article "Rubin," in *Philosophical Encyclopedia* (Moscow, 1967), vol. 4, p. 529.

20. See V. A. Rubin, "On the Dating and Authenticity of the *Tso Chuan,*" *Problemy vostokovedeniia,* 1959, No. 1, pp. 78–85; "Slaveholding in Ancient China in the 7th–5th Centuries B.C.," *Vestnik drevnei istorii,* 1959, no. 3, pp. 3–21; "The People's Assembly in Ancient China," *Vestnik drevnei istorii,* 1960, no. 4, pp. 22–40; "Tzu ch'an and the City-State of Ancient China," *T'oung Pao,* liii, 1–3, 1965, pp. 8–34.

21. Peking University and Tsinghua University Group for Mass Criticism, "Dead Soul of Confucius, Fond Dream of New Tsars," *Peking Review,* no. 6, February 8, 1974.

22. Only very recently, during the course of the polemics with the Chinese, has the position of Soviet sinologists changed somewhat, and in the Soviet press there have appeared materials containing condemnations of Mao Tse-tung because he exalts Ch'in Shih-huang. See Wang Ming, "Great Disorders in the Realm of the Great Helmsman," *Za rubezhom,* 1974, no. 20, pp. 14–16.

23. "Dead Soul of Confucius . . .," pp. 13–14.

24. See note 18 above, p. 75.

### 1. Tradition and human personality

1. For the most part we shall refer to these city-states as kingdoms.

2. Vitaly A. Rubin, "The People's Assembly in Ancient China," *Vestnik drevnei istorii* [Review of Ancient History], 1960, no. 4 (in Russian).

3. Bernhard Karlgren, "The Book of Documents," *Bulletin of the Museum of Far Eastern Antiquities,* vol. 22 (Stockholm, 1950) p. 10 (modified).

4. James Legge, *The Chinese Classics, with a translation, critical and exegetical notes,* vol. 5 (Hong Kong, 1960), p. 47 (modified).

5. *Ibid.,* p. 462 (modified).

6. *Kuo Yü* (Shanghai, 1958), p. 44 (in Chinese).

7. James Legge, trans. *The Four Books, Confucian Analects* (New York: Paragon Reprint Corp., 1966), p. 162, XII:7 (modified).

8. M. V. Kriukov, *Formy sotsialnoi organizatsii drevnikh kitaitsev* [Forms of Social Organisation of Ancient Chinese People] (Moscow, 1967) (in Russian).

9. Legge, *The Four Books, The Works of Mencius,* pp. 841–42, VI:7.

10. Vitaly A. Rubin, "How Ssu-ma Ch'ien Depicted the 'Spring and Autumn' Era," *Narody Azii i Afriki* [Peoples of Asia and Africa], 1966, no. 2, p. 85 (in Russian).

11. H. G. Creel, *Confucius: The Man and The Myth* (London: Routledge, 1951).

12. Legge, *Confucian Analects,* p. 123, X:2.

13. *Ibid.,* p. 182, XIII:14.

14. Creel, *Confucius: Man and Myth,* p. 60.

15. Arthur Waley, trans., *The Analects of Confucius* (New York: Macmillan, 1938), pp. 104–5, IV:14.

16. Legge, *Analects,* pp. 83–84, VII:13.

17. Waley, *Analects,* p. 131, VII:37.

18. A. L. Kroeber and Clyde Kluckhohn, *The Concept of Culture: A Critical Review of Definitions* (New York: Vintage, 1965).

19. Jan Szczepanski, *Elementarnye poniatiia sotsiologii* [Elementary Concepts of Sociology] (Moscow, 1969), p. 39 (Russian translation).

20. *Ibid.,* p. 42.

21. Yu. M. Lotman, "On the Problem of the Typology of Culture," *Studies in Semiotic Systems,* vol. 3 (Tartu, 1967), p. 30.

22. D. S. Likhachev, *Poetika drevnerusskoi literatury* [The Poetics of Old Russian Literature] (Leningrad, 1967), pp. 97, 100.

23. Yu. M. Lotman, "On the Contrast between 'Honor' and 'Glory' in Secular Texts of the Kievan Era," *Trudy po znakovym sistemam* [Studies in Semiotic Systems], vol. 3, p. 102 (in Russian).

24. Seraphin Couvreur, *Li Ki ou memoires sur les bienséances et les cérémonies* [Li ki or Notes on Etiquette and Ceremony] (Paris, 1950), pp. 94–95.

25. *Ibid.,* p. 105.

26. Bernhard Karlgren, "Grammata Serica Recensa," *Bulletin of the Museum of Far Eastern Antiquities,* vol. 22 (Stockholm, 1957), p. 130.

27. Waley, *Analects,* p. 139 (modified), IX:5.

28. Wolfgang Bauer, "China: Verwirklichungen einer Utopie," *Propiläen Weltgeschichte,* vol. 11 (Berlin, 1965), p. 143.

29. N. I. Konrad, *Zapad i Vostok* [West and East] (Moscow, 1966), p. 60 (in Russian).

30. E. Chavannes, *Les Mémoires Historiques de Se-ma Ts'ien,* vol. 1 (Paris, 1895), p. 217.

31. Thus in the "Wen-hou chih ming," a part of the *Shu ching* dating from the beginning of the eighth century b.c., the following words are put into the mouth of King P'ing of Chou: "The glorious Wen and Wu by their efforts succeeded in having their shining virtues elevated to on high and broadly dispersed below" (cf. Legge, *The Chinese Classics,* vol. 3, p. 613).

32. Legge, *The Chinese Classics,* vol. 5, p. 433.

33. Waley, *Analects,* p. 84, I:6 (modified).

34. In European languages one can find a certain analogous contrast between war and culture. Along with its meaning of "civilian" (as opposed to military), the word "civil" in both French and English also signifies politeness and education.

35. Cf. Fung Yu-lan, *A History of Chinese Philosophy,* trans. by Derk Bodde, vol. 2 (Princeton: Princeton University Press, 1953), p. 69.

36. Waley, *Analects,* p. 89, II:7.

37. *Ibid.,* pp. 88–89, II:5.

38. *Ibid.,* Introduction, p. 54.

39. Couvreur, *Li Ki,* p. 622.

40. Hsie Yu-wei, "Filial Piety and Chinese Society," in *The Chinese Mind: Essentials of Chinese Philosophy and Culture,* eds. Charles A. Moore and A. V. Morris (Honolulu: University of Hawaii Press, 1967), pp. 174–75.

41. Waley, *Analects,* p. 176, XIII:20.

42. *Ibid.,* p. 111, V:15.

43. *Ibid.,* p. 83, I:2.

44. Etienne Balazs, *Chinese Civilisation and Bureaucracy,* trans. H. M. Wright (New Haven: Yale University Press, 1964), p. 18.

45. Waley, *Analects*, p. 88, II:3.

46. Legge, *The Chinese Classics*, vol. 5, p. 730.

47. H. G. Creel, *Confucius: Man and Myth*, p. 175.

48. Vitaly A. Rubin, "On the Dating and Authenticity of the *Tso chuan*," *Problemy Vostokovedeniia* [Problems of Orientology], 1959, no. 1, p. 85 (in Russian).

49. F. A. Sinclair, *A History of Greek Political Thought* (London: Routledge and Paul, 1952), p. 35.

50. Cf. *The Dialogues of Plato*, trans. by B. Jowett (Oxford: Clarendon Press, 1953), vol. 4, pp. 273–75.

51. Waley, *Analects*, p. 186, XIV:23 (modified).

52. *Ibid.*, pp. 163–64, XII:5 (modified).

53. *Ibid.*, p. 103, IV:5 (modified).

54. *Ibid.*, p. 195, XV:8.

55. *Ibid.*, p. 87, I:14.

56. *Ibid.*, pp. 103–4, IV:9.

57. Legge, *Analects*, p. 44, IV:16.

58. Recently a new interpretation of *yi* has been given in the article by Chung-ying Cheng, "On *yi* as a Universal Principle of Specific Application in Confucian Morality," *Philosophy East and West*, vol. 24, no. 3 (July 1972).

59. Legge, *Analects*, p. 171, XII:22.

60. Waley, *Analects*, p. 162, XII:2.

61. *Ibid.*, pp. 84–85, I:7.

62. *Ibid.*, p. 84, I:6.

63. *Ibid.*, p. 183, XIV:3.

64. *Ibid.*, p. 177, XIII:21.

65. *Ibid.*, p. 132, VIII:2.

66. *Ibid.*, pp. 211–12, XVII:8 (modified).

67. *Ibid.*, p. 140, IX:10.

68. Dialogue *Timaeus*, 87c–89d, cf. *The Dialogues of Plato*, trans. Jowett, vol. 3, pp. 775–77.

69. Cf. W. Scott Morton, "The Confucian Concept of Man: the Original Formulation," *Philosophy East and West*, vol. 31, no. 1 (January 1971), p. 74.

70. Plato's dialogues *Gorgias*, 470e, and *Laches*, 192c (cf. *The Dialogues of Plato*, vol. 2, p. 560; vol. 1, p. 87); Aristotle's *Metaphysics*, 1072 B 13 ff.

71. *Aristoteles Hauptwerke*, Leipzig, 1934, p. 74.

72. Aristotle, *Nichomachean Ethics*, trans. with an introduction and notes by Martin Oswald (Indianapolis and New York: Library of Liberal Arts, 1962), p. 111, book V, 1129a:1–5.

73. Konrad, *Zapad i Vostok*, p. 293.

74. Waley, *Analects*, p. 90, II:12 (modified).

75. Leon Vandermeersch, *La formation du légisme* (Paris, 1965), p. 247.

76. F. S. Bykov, *Zarozhdeniie politicheskoi i filosofskoi mysli v Kitae* [The Origin of Political and Philosophical Thought in China] (Moscow, 1966), p. 98 (in Russian).

77. Waley, *Analects*, p. 139, IX:5.

78. *Ibid.*, p. 155, IX:11.

79. Cf. Etienne Balazs, *Chinese Civilisation and Bureaucracy*, pp. 18–19; Wolfram Eberhard, *A History of China* (Berkeley and Los Angeles: University of California Press, 1950), pp. 41–42; Henri Maspero and Etienne Balazs, *Histoire et institutions de la Chine ancienne* (Paris, 1967), pp. 30–31.

80. Waley, *Analects*, p. 194, XV:6.

81. *Ibid.*, p. 180, XIV:1.

82. Legge, *Analects*, p. 188, XIII:23. I adhere to the interpretation given by John C. H. Wu in his article "The Status of the Individual in the Political and Legal Traditions of Old and New China," *The Chinese Mind*, p. 343.

83. Burton Watson, *The Complete Works of Chuang Tzu* (New York: Columbia University Press, 1968), p. 54.

84. *Ibid.*, pp. 54–58.

85. Paul Demieville, "Aperçu historique des études sinologiques en France," *Acta Asiatica* [Historical Sketch of Sinological Studies in France], Tokyo, 1966, no. 11, p. 63.

86. Robert M. Marsh, *The Mandarins* (Glencoe: Free Press, 1961); Ho Ping-ti, *The Ladder of Success in Imperial China* (New York: Columbia University Press, 1963).

87. Cf. Leon Vandermeersch, *La formation du légisme*; Vitaly A. Rubin, "Traditions of Chinese Political Thought," *Voprosy Filosofii* [Problems of Philosophy], 1970, no. 5 (in Russian).

## 2. "State machine for the general welfare"

1. Fung Yu-lan, *A History of Chinese Philosophy,* trans. by Derk Bodde, vol. 1 (Princeton: Princeton University Press, 1953), p. 76 (modified).

2. Burton Watson, trans. *Mo Tzu: Basic Writings* (New York: Columbia University Press, 1963), p. 112.

3. James Legge, *The Four Books. The Works of Mencius* (New York: Paragon Reprint Corp., 1966), p. 678, III B:9:9.

4. Ernst Faber, *Grundgedanken des alten chinesischen Sozialismus oder Lehre des Philosophen Micius* (Elberfeldt, 1877), p. 5.

5. Alexandra David, *Socialisme chinoise. Le philosophe Meh-Ti et l'idée de solidarité* (Paris, 1907), p. vii.

6. Leon Wieger, *A History of the Religious Beliefs and Philosophical Opinions in China from the Beginning to the Present Time,* trans. Edward C. Werner (Hsien-hsien, 1927), p. 209.

7. Alfred Forke, *Geschichte der alten chinesischen Philosophie* (Hamburg, 1927), p. 394.

8. Burton Watson, *Mo Tzu,* p. 39.

9. *Ibid.,* pp. 39–40 (modified).

10. Fung Yu-lan, *Chinese Philosophy,* vol. 1, p. 91.

11. Cf. Burton Watson, trans. *The Complete Works of Chuang Tzu* (New York: Columbia University Press, 1968), pp. 365–66.

12. Burton Watson, *Mo Tzu,* pp. 46–47.

13. *Ibid.,* p. 49.

14. Leon Vandermeersch, *La formation du légisme* (Paris, 1965), p. 211.

15. Etienne Balazs, *Chinese Civilization and Bureaucracy,* trans. H. M. Wright (New Haven: Yale University Press, 1964).

16. Burton Watson, *Mo Tzu,* pp. 46–47.

17. *Ibid.,* p. 49.

18. Thomas Hobbes, *Leviathan or the Matter, Form and Power of a Commonwealth Ecclesiastical and Civil* (Oxford: Basil Blackwell, 1960), p. 110.

19. Burton Watson, *Mo Tzu,* pp. 34–36.

20. Marcel Granet considers that this conformism is more terrible than the Legalist because "for the Legalists it sufficed that the ruler dictated laws. But for Mo Tzu he must dictate opinion." *La pensée chinoise* (Paris, 1934), p. 494.

21. See chapter 6 of *Han Fei Tzu* where it is said: "Those who defy their sovereign or oppose him with strong censure, I would not call loyal." Burton Watson, trans. *Han Fei Tzu: Basic Writings* (New York: Columbia University Press, 1964), p. 25.

22. Legge, *Confucian Analects*, pp. 184–85 (modified).

23. To be sure, in chapter 13 of *Mo Tzu* there is mention of the family, but this changes nothing because the family, as that passage emphasizes, is not at all differentiated from all-under-Heaven and the kingdom. It must be ruled by the same methods.

24. Burton Watson, *Mo Tzu*, p. 36.

25. *Ibid.*, p. 38.

26. Seraphin Couvreur, *Li Ki ou mémoires sur les bienséances et les cérémonies*, p. 498.

27. Mei Yi-pao, *The Ethical and Political Works of Motse* (London, 1929) p. 224 (modified).

28. Burton Watson, *Mo Tzu*, p. 18.

29. *Ibid.*, p. 19.

30. *Ibid.*, pp. 22–23.

31. Basing their arguments on a notion of Mo Tzu as a moralist, some sinologists give this term a moral meaning; they interpret it as "noble," "wise" etc. My conception is based on the meaning of the term in the context of *Mo Tzu*. This meaning is encountered in the *Lun yü* as well, where there is a section (XIV:33) in which *hsien* is defined as a man who, without knowing that others intend to deceive him, still intuits this before others do. Cf. Legge, *Confucian Analects*, p. 209.

32. Burton Watson, *Mo Tzu*, pp. 23–24 slightly modified.

33. *Ibid.*, p. 24.

34. *Ibid.*, p. 25.

35. *Ibid.*, p. 28.

36. *Ibid.*, p. 126.

37. H. G. Creel, *Chinese Thought from Confucius to Mao Tse-tung* (Chicago: University of Chicago Press, 1953).

38. Arthur Waley, trans., *The Analects of Confucius* (New York: Macmillan, 1938), p. 190, XIV:41.

39. Burton Watson, *Mo Tzu*, p. 39.

40. This is an almost exact reproduction of Confucius' self-characterization. Cf. Waley, *Analects*, p. 123, VII:1.

41. Burton Watson, *Mo Tzu*, pp. 127–28.

42. Several contemporary thinkers advocate a similar view. Stanislaw Lem writes: "There is a widespread belief among humanists that the existence of problems which cannot be solved experimentally makes them similar to gamblers who, playing their cards now this way and now that, have been playing one and the same game since the beginning of time. The cards change but the round drags on, and there is no end to it. . . . In other words, century after century humanists keep shuffling their cards while the empiricists have something developing: they have a real increase in information." Stanislaw Lem, "A Model of Culture," *Voprosy Filosofii* [Problems of Philosophy], 1969, no. 8, p. 50 (in Russian).

43. Burton Watson, *Mo Tzu*, p. 63.

44. *Ibid.*, p. 110.

45. *Ibid.*, p. 111.

46. *Ibid.*, p. 114.

47. Fung Yu-lan, *Chinese Philosophy*, vol. 1, p. 90.

48. Mei Yi-pao, *Works of Motse*, pp. 28–29.

49. *Ibid.*, p. 235.

50. *Ibid.*, pp. 235–36.

51. *Ibid.*, p. 237.

52. Henri Maspero, *La Chine Antique* (Paris, 1965), p. 448.

53. A. Forke, *Alten chinesischen Philosophie*, p. 368.

54. Edwin O. Reischauer and John King Fairbank, *East Asia: The Great Tradition* (Boston: Houghton Mifflin, 1960), p. 79.

55. Burton Watson, *Mo Tzu*, "Introduction," p. 13.

### 3. The theory and practice of a totalitarian state

1. J. J. L. Duyvendak, *The Book of Lord Shang: A Classic of the Chinese School of Law* (Chicago: University of Chicago Press, 1963); W. K. Liao, *The Complete Works of Han Fei Tzu*, vols. 1–2 (London: Probsthain, 1959); L. S. Perelomov, *Kniga pravitelia oblasti Shan* [The Book of the Ruler of Shang District] (Moscow, 1968) (in Russian).

2. Leon Vandermeersch, *La formation du légisme* (Paris, 1965), p. 277.

3. Recently after investigating the question of Shen Tao's relation to Legalist theory I came to the conclusion that in fact this thinker has nothing in common with it. See Vitaly Rubin, "Shen Tao and Fa-chia," JAOS, vol. 94 (July–Sept. 1974), pp. 337–46.

4. H. G. Creel, "The Fa-chia: 'Legalists' or 'Administrators'?," *What is Taoism? and Other Studies in Chinese Cultural History* (Chicago and London: University of Chicago Press, 1970), pp. 92–120.

5. Duyvendak, *Book of Lord Shang*, p. 13.

6. *Ibid.*, pp. 14–15.

7. *Ibid.*, p. 17.

8. *Ibid.*, pp. 30–31 (slightly modified).

9. *Ibid.*, p. 145.

10. Perelomov, trans. *Book of the Ruler of Shang District*, p. 32.

11. Duyvendak, *Lord Shang*, p. 178.

12. *Ibid.*, p. 285.

13. George H. Sabine, *A History of Political Theory* (New York: Henry Holt and Co., 1950), p. 343.

14. Duyvendak, *Book of Lord Shang*, p. 303.

15. *Ibid.*, p. 216.

16. *Ibid.*, p. 285.

17. *Ibid.*, p. 262.

18. Liao, *Works of Han Fei Tzu*, vol. 1, p. 270.

19. James Legge, *The Four Books, The Works of Mencius* (New York: Paragon Reprint Corp., 1966), pp. 493–94, I B:8.

20. Duyvendak, *Book of Lord Shang*, p. 223.

21. *Ibid.*, p. 217.

22. Cf. Liao, *Works of Han Fei Tzu*, vol. 2, p. 239.

23. Duyvendak, *Book of Lord Shang*, p. 312.

24. *Ibid.*, p. 288.

25. *Ibid.*, p. 225.

26. Waley, *Analects*, p. 88, II:3.

27. Duyvendak, *Book of Lord Shang*, p. 89.

28. *Ibid.*, p. 81.

29. Derk Bodde and Clarence Morris, *Law in Imperial China* (Cambridge, Mass.: Harvard University Press, 1967), p. 9.

30. Burton Watson, trans., *Han Fei Tzu: Basic Writings* (New York: Columbia University Press, 1964), pp. 30–34.

31. Duyvendak, *Book of Lord Shang*, p. 230.

32. *Ibid.*, pp. 201–2.

33. Cf. W. K. Liao, *Works of Han Fei Tzu*, vol. 2, p. 326.

34. Duyvendak, *Book of Lord Shang*, p. 208.

35. *Ibid.*, p. 229.

36. *Ibid.*, pp. 229–30.

37. Cf. Liao, *Works of Han Fei Tzu*, vol. 1, pp. 29–30.

38. Duyvendak, *Book of Lord Shang*, p. 281 (modified).

39. *Ibid.*, p. 231 (modified).

40. *Ibid.*, p. 232 (modified).

41. Watson, *Han Fei Tzu*, pp. 105–6.

42. Derk Bodde and Clarence Morris, *Law in Imperial China*, p. 40.

43. Duyvendak, *Book of Lord Shang*, p. 282.

44. *Ibid.*, p. 283.

45. Cf. Liao, *Works of Han Fei Tzu*, vol. 2, pp. 215–16.

46. Duyvendak, *Book of Lord Shang*, p. 90.

47. See, for example, the first chapter of the *Shang-chün shu*, "the Reform of the Law," where it is said that the ancient kings established laws in accordance with the demands of the times. Cf. Duyvendak, *Book of Lord Shang*, pp. 172–73.

48. Vandermeersch, *Formation du légisme*, p. 192.

49. Duyvendak, *Book of Lord Shang*, p. 192.

50. *Ibid.*, pp. 193–94.

51. *Ibid.*, p. 184.

52. *Ibid.*, p. 178.

53. *Ibid.*, pp. 178–79.

54. *Ibid.*, p. 181.

55. *Ibid.*, p. 177.

56. *Ibid.*, p. 191.

57. *Ibid.*

58. *Ibid.*, pp. 206–7.

59. *Ibid.*, p. 195 (slightly modified).

60. *Ibid.*, p. 282.

61. *Ibid.*, p. 191.

62. *Ibid.*, pp. 188–89.

63. *Ibid.*, p. 194.

64. Cf. Liao, *Works of Han Fei Tzu*, vol. 2, p. 33.

65. *Ibid.*

66. *Ibid.*, p. 34.

67. Duyvendak, *Book of Lord Shang*, p. 196 (slightly modified).

68. D. Granin, "Two images," *Novyi mir* [New World], 1968, no. 3, p. 224.

69. Duyvendak, *Book of Lord Shang*, p. 190.

70. *Ibid.*, p. 199.

71. *Ibid.*, pp. 253–54.

72. E. Chavannes, *Les Mémoires Historiques de Se-ma Ts'ien*, vol. 1 (Paris, 1895) p. 225.

73. Cf. Kuo Mo-jo, "Shu Wu Ch'i," *Ch'ing t'ung shih tai* [The Bronze Age] (Peking, 1954), pp. 202–30 (in Chinese).

74. Burton Watson, *Hsün Tzu: Basic Writings* (New York: Columbia University Press, 1963), p. 64.

75. Burton Watson, *Early Chinese Literature* (New York: Columbia University Press, 1962), p. 177.

76. Legge, *The Works of Mencius*, p. 708, IV A:10.

77. *Ibid.*, p. 948, VII A:20.

78. *Ibid.*, p. 597, II B:12.

79. *Ibid.*, p. 464, I A:7.

80. Subsequently Meng Tzu's idea exerted immense influence on the development of utopian thought in China. The question of the actual and ideological roots of the "ching t'ien system" has been a topic of lively discussion among sinologists.

81. Legge, *The Works of Mencius*, pp. 482–83, I B:4.

82. *Ibid.*, pp. 760–61, IV B:29.

83. *Ibid.*, p. 714, IV A:14.

84. Meng Tzu described the administration of the ideal king Wen-wang of Chou as follows: "Cultivators were taxed the ninth part of the harvest; the descendants of officials were given stipends; at the passes and in the markets, goods were inspected, but not taxed; there were no prohibitions respecting the ponds and weirs; the wives and children of criminals were not involved in their guilt. Poor people—widows, widowers,

orphans and the childless—had no one in all-under-Heaven to tell of their wants. But Wen-wang gave them first consideration in his humane government" (cf. Legge, *The Works of Mencius*, pp. 485–86, I B:5).

85. *Ibid.*, p. 445, IA:5.

86. *Ibid.*, p. 1000, VII B:31.

87. *Ibid.*, pp. 446–48, I A:6.

88. *Ibid.*, p. 984, VII B:13.

89. Watson, *Hsün Tzu*, p. 76.

90. Homer H. Dubs, *The Works of Hsüntze* (London: Arthur Probsthain, 1928), p. 193.

91. Burton Watson, *Han Fei Tzu*, pp. 120–21.

92. *Ibid.*, p. 128.

93. Cf. Sabine, *History of Political Theory*, p. 59.

94. Aristotle, *The Politics*, trans. Rackham (Cambridge, Mass.: Harvard University Press, Loeb Classical Library, 1959), p. 227, III:vi:9–10.

95. Liao, *Works of Han Fei Tzu*, vol. 1, p. 31.

96. *Ibid.*, p. 32.

97. N. I. Konrad, *Sun Tzu* (Moscow, 1950), p. 34 (in Russian).

98. Legge, *The Works of Mencius*, p. 588, II B:9.

99. Dubs, *Works of Hsüntze*, pp. 187–88.

100. Burton Watson, *Han Fei Tzu*, p. 82.

101. *Ibid.*, p. 111.

## 4. Nature against civilization

1. Arthur Waley, *The Analects of Confucius* (New York: Macmillan, 1938), pp. 220–21, XVIII: 7.

2. *Ibid.*

3. *Ibid.*, p. 222, XVIII: 8.

4. Arthur Waley, *The Way and Its Power: A Study of the Tao Te Ching and Its Place in Chinese Thought* (New York: Macmillan, 1958), p. 174.

5. Cf. Fung Yu-lan, *A History of Chinese Philosophy*, trans. by Derk Bodde (Princeton: Princeton University Press, 1953), vol. 1, p. 221.

6. Burton Watson, *The Complete Works of Chuang Tzu* (New York: Columbia University Press, 1968), p. 357 (hereinafter cited as Watson, *CWCT*).

7. *Ibid.*, p. 216.

8. *Ibid.*, pp. 373–74.

9. *Ibid.*, pp. 86–87.

10. Cf. *ibid.*, p. 78.

11. *Ibid.*, p. 148.

12. *Ibid.*, pp. 149–50 modified. (Dr. Rubin prefers "humanity and justice" to Watson's "benevolence and righteousness"—trans.).

13. *Ibid.*, p. 163.

14. *Ibid.*, p. 87.

15. *Ibid.*, p. 58.

16. *Ibid.*, p. 90.

17. I. S. Kon, *Sotsiologiia lichnosti* [The Sociology of Personality] (Moscow, 1967), p. 7 (in Russian).

18. *Ibid.*, p. 29.

19. Watson, *CWCT*, pp. 63–64.

20. *Ibid.*, p. 67.

21. Henri Maspero, *Mélanges posthumes sur les réligions et l'histoire de la Chine* (Paris, 1950), vol. 2, pp. 72–222.

22. Wolfgang Bauer, "Icherleben und Autobiographie in älteren China," [First-person Experience and Autobiography in Ancient China] *Heidelberger Jahrbücher* (Heidelberg, 1964), no. 8, pp. 15–17.

23. Waley, *The Way and Its Power*, p. 169.

24. Watson, *CWCT*, p. 99.

25. Legge, *The Works of Mencius*, p. 850, VI A: 1.

26. Watson, *CWCT*, pp. 78–79.

27. *Ibid.*, p. 94.

28. *Ibid.*, pp. 101–2.

29. *Ibid.*, pp. 108–9.

30. *Ibid.*, pp. 98–99.

31. *Ibid.*, p. 39.

32. Waley, *The Way and Its Power*, p. 143.

33. Watson, *CWCT*, pp. 152–53.

34. *Ibid.*, p. 134.

35. *Ibid.*, pp. 135–36.

36. *Ibid.*, pp. 116–18.

37. *Ibid.*, p. 104.

38. *Ibid.*, p. 105.

39. *Ibid.*, p. 112.

40. Yu. M. Lotman, "On the Problem of the Typology of Culture," *Studies in Semiotic Systems,* vol. 3 (Tartu, 1967), pp. 36, 37.

41. A. Losev, "Diogenes," *Filosofskaia Entsiklopediia* [Philosophical Encyclopedia] (Moscow, 1962), vol. 3, p. 18 (in Russian).

42. Jean-Jacques Rousseau, "Discourse on the Origin of Inequality," *The Social Contract and Other Writings,* G. D. H. Cole editor (London: Dutton, Everyman Library Edition, 1973), pp. 243–44.

43. *Ibid.*, p. 234.

44. Watson, *CWCT,* p. 113.

45. *Ibid.*, pp. 110–11.

46. Wang Wei, "Introduction to Painting," Wm. Theodore de Bary et al., compilers, *Sources of Chinese Tradition* (New York: Columbia University Press, 1964), vol. 1, p. 255.

# SELECT BIBLIOGRAPHY

## Chinese sources in translation

Couvreur, Seraphin. *Li ki ou mémoires sur les bienséances et les cérémonies* [Li Ki or Notes on Etiquette and Ceremony]. Paris: Cathasia, 1950.

Dubs, Homer H. *The Works of Hsüntse*. London: Arthur Probsthain, 1928.

Duyvendak, J. J. L. *The Book of Lord Shang: A Classic of the Chinese School of Law*. Chicago: University of Chicago Press, 1963.

Karlgren, Bernhard. *The Book of Documents*. Bulletin of the Museum of Far Eastern Antiquities, no. 22. Stockholm, 1950.

Lau, D. C. *Mencius*. Harmondsworth, England: Penguin, 1970.

Legge, James. *The Chinese Classics, with a translation, critical and exegetical notes*. Hong Kong, 1960, vol. 5.

———— *The Four Books*. (Reprint of 1923 Shanghai edition.) New York: Paragon Book Reprint Corp., 1966.

Liao, W. K. *The Complete Works of Han Fei Tzu*. London: Arthur Probsthain, 1959.

Mei Yi-pao. *The Ethical and Political Works of Motse*. London: Arthur Probsthain, 1929.

Waley, Arthur. *The Analects of Confucius*. New York: Macmillan, 1938.

———— *The Way and Its Power: A Study of the Tao Te Ching and Its Place in Chinese Thought*. New York: Macmillan, 1958.

Watson, Burton. *The Complete Works of Chuang Tzu*. New York: Columbia University Press, 1964.

———— *Han Fei Tzu: Basic Writings*. New York: Columbia University Press, 1964.

———— *Hsün Tzu: Basic Writings*. New York: Columbia University Press, 1963.

———— *Mo Tzu: Basic Writings*. New York: Columbia University Press, 1963.

## Other sources

Aristotle. *Nichomachean Ethics*. Translated, with an introduction and notes by Martin Oswald. Indianapolis and New York: Bobbs-Merrill, 1962.

Aristotle. *The Politics*. Trans. H. Rackman. Cambridge, Mass.: Harvard University Press, Loeb Classical Library, 1959.

Balazs, Etienne. *Chinese Civilization and Bureaucracy*. Trans. H. M. Wright. New Haven: Yale University Press, 1964.

Bauer, Wolfgang. "China: Verwirklichungen einer Utopie" [China: The Realization of a Utopia]. *Propiläen Weltgeschichte*. Berlin, 1965, vol. 5.

——— "Icherleben und Autobiographie in älteren China" [First-person Experience and Autobiography in Ancient China]. *Heidelberger Jahrbücher*. Heidelberg, 1964, no. 8.

Bodde, Derk, and Clarence Morris, eds. *Law in Imperial China*. Cambridge, Mass.: Harvard University Press, 1967.

Bykov, F. S. *Zarozhdenie politicheskoi i filosofskoi mysli v Kitae* [The Origin of Political and Philosophical Thought in China]. Moscow, 1966.

Creel, Herrlee Glessner. *Chinese Thought from Confucius to Mao Tse-tung*. Chicago: University of Chicago Press, 1953.

——— *Confucius, The Man and the Myth*. London: Routledge, 1951.

David, Alexandra. *Socialisme chinois. La philosophie Meh-Ti et l'idée de solidarité* [Chinese Socialism. The Philosophy of Meh Ti and the Idea of Solidarity]. London: Luzac and Co., 1907.

de Bary, Wm. Theodore, et al., compilers. *Sources of Chinese Tradition*. New York: Columbia University Press, 1960.

Demiéville, Paul. "Aperçu historique des études sinologiques en France" [Historical Sketch of Sinological Studies in France]. *Acta Asiatica*. Tokyo, 1966. No. 11.

Faber, E. *Grundgedanken des alten chinesischen Sozialismus oder Lehre des Philosophen Micius* [Fundamental Ideas of Ancient Chinese Socialism or the Teachings of the Philosopher Micius]. Elberfeldt: R. L. Friderichs, 1877.

Forke, Alfred. *Geschichte der alten chinesischen Philosophie* [History of Ancient Chinese Philosophy]. Hamburg: Kommissionersverlag L. Friederichsen & Co., 1927.

Franke, Herbert. "Max Webers Soziologie der ostasiatischen Religionen." *Max Weber. Gedächtnisschrift der Ludwig-Maximilian-Universität. München* [Max Weber's Sociology of East Asian Religion. Essays in Honor of Max Weber from the Ludwig-Maximiliam University, Munich]. Berlin, 1966.

Fung Yu-lan. *A History of Chinese Philosophy*. Trans. Derk Bodde. Vol. 1, Princeton: Princeton University Press, 1952.

Granet, Marcel. *La pensée chinoise* [Chinese Thought]. Paris: La Renaissance du livre, 1934.

Granin, D. "Dva lika" [Two Images]. *Novyi Mir*. 1968, no. 3.

Ho Ping-ti. *The Ladder of Success in Imperial China*. New York: Columbia University Press, 1963.

Hobbes, Thomas. *Leviathan or the Matter, Forme and Power of a Commonwealth Ecclesiastical and Civil.* Edited with an introduction by Michael Oakeshott. Oxford: Basil Blackwell, 1960.

Hsieh Yu-wei. "Filial Piety and Chinese Society." In *The Chinese Mind,* ed. Charles A. Moore. Honolulu: East-West Center Press, 1967.

Karlgren, Bernhard. "Grammata Serica Recensa." *Bulletin of the Museum of Far Eastern Antiquities,* vol. 29. Stockholm, 1957.

Kon, I. S. *Sotsiologiia lichnosti* [The Sociology of Personality]. Moscow, 1967.

Konrad, N. I. *Zapad i vostok* [West and East]. Moscow, 1966.

—— *Sun-tzy* [Hsün-tzu]. Moscow, 1950.

Kroeber, A. L., and C. Kluckhohn. *The Concept of Culture, a Critical Review of Definitions.* New York: Vintage, 1965.

Kryukov, M. V. *Formy sotsial'noi organizatsii drevnikh kitaitsev* [Forms of Social Organization among the Ancient Chinese]. Moscow, 1967.

Kuo Mo-jo. *Bronzovyi vek* [The Bronze Age]. Moscow, 1959.

Lem, Stanislaw. "Model' kul'tury" [A Model of Culture]. *Voprosy filosofii.* No. 8, 1969.

Likhachev, D. S. *Poetika drevnerusskoi literatury* [The Poetics of Old Russian Literature]. Leningrad, 1967.

Losev, A. "Diogen" [Diogenes]. *Filosofskaya entsiklopediia.* Vol. 2, Moscow, 1962.

Lotman, Yu. M. "Ob oppozitsii 'chest'—'slava' v svetskikh tekstakh kievskogo perioda" [On the Distinction between the Terms 'Honor' and 'Fame' in Secular Texts of the Kievan Era]. *Trudy po znakovym sistemam.* Vol. 3, Tartu, 1967.

Marsh, Robert M. *The Mandarins.* Glencoe, Ill.: The Free Press, 1961.

Maspero, Henri. *La Chine antique* [Ancient China]. Paris: E. de Boccard, 1927.

—— *Mélanges posthumes sur les réligions et l'histoire de la Chine* [Posthumous Miscellany on the Religion and History of China]. Vol. 2, Paris: Civilisation du Sud, 1950.

Perelomov, L. S. trans. *Kniga pravitelia oblasti Shang* [The Book of the Ruler of Shang District]. Moscow, 1968.

—— "O roli ideologii v stanovlenii despoticheskogo gosudarstva v drevnem Kitae" [On the Role of Ideology in the Formation of a Despotic State in Ancient China]. *Narody Azii i Afriki,* 1967, no. 3.

Plato. *The Laws.* Cambridge, Mass.: Harvard University Press, 1961.

Pozdneeva, L. D. trans. *Ateisty, materialisty i dialektiki drevnego Kitaia* [Atheists, Materialists and Dialecticians in Ancient China]. Moscow, 1967.

Reischauer, Edwin O., and John King Fairbank. *East Asia: The Great Tradition.* Boston: Houghton, Mifflin, 1960.

Rousseau, Jean-Jacques. *The Social Contract and Discourses.* Translated and edited by G. D. H. Cole. London: Dutton, Everyman Library Edition, 1973.

Rubin, Vitaly A. "Kak Syma Tsian' izobrazhal period Chun'tsyu," [How Ssu-Ma Ch'ien Depicted the 'Spring and Autumn' Era]. *Narody Azii i Afriki*, 1966, no. 2.

—— "Dva istoka kitaiskoi politicheskoi mysli" [Two Currents of Chinese Political Thought]. *Voprosy istorii*, 1967, no. 3.

—— "O datirovke i autentichnosti 'Tso chzhuan' " [On the Dating and Authenticity of the *Tso Chuan*]. *Problemy vostokovedeniia*, 1959, no. 1.

—— trans. "Zapiski o muzyke" [Notes on Music]. *Muzykal'naya estetika stran Vostoka*. Moscow, 1967.

Sabine, George H. *A History of Political Theory*. New York: Henry Holt & Co., 1950.

Sinclair, F. A. *A History of Greek Political Thought*. London: Routledge & Paul, 1952.

Szczepanski, Jan. *Elementarnye poniatiia sotsiologii* [Elementary Concepts of Sociology]. Moscow, 1969.

Vandermeersch, Leon. *La formation du légisme* [The Formation of Legalism]. Paris: École française d'extrême orient, 1965.

Vasiliev, L. S. "Problema tszintian' " [The Problem of the Well-Field]. *Kitai i iaponiia. K semidesiatiletiiu Akad. N. I. Konrad*. Moscow, 1961.

Watson, Burton. *Early Chinese Literature*. New York: Columbia University Press, 1962.

Weber, Max. *Gesammelte Aufsätze zur Religionssoziologie* [Collected Articles on the Sociology of Religion]. Vol. 1, Tübingen, 1920.

Wieger, Leon. *A History of the Religious Beliefs and Philosophical Opinions in China from the Beginning to the Present Time*, trans. Edward C. Werner. Hsien-hsien, 1927.

Yang Hsing-shun. *Drevnekitaiskii filosof Lao-tszy i ego ucheniie* [The Ancient Chinese Philosopher Lao Tzu and His Teaching]. Moscow and Leningrad, 1950.

# THE WRITINGS OF
# VITALY A. RUBIN

## Book

*Ideologiia i kul'tura drevnego Kitaia* (*Chetyre silueta*) [Ideology and Culture In Ancient China: Four Silhouettes—the literal Russian translation of the present volume]. Moscow: Nauka, 1970.

## Articles

"Shen Tao and Fa-Chia." In *Journal of the American Oriental Society* 94, no. 3 (July–September 1974): 337–46.

"The End of Confucianism?" In *T'oung Pao,* 59 (1973): 68–78.

"Traditsii kitaiskoi politicheskoi mysli" [Traditions of Chinese Political Thought]. In *Voprosy Filosofii* [Problems of Philosophy] 5 (1970): 90–101.

"Chelovek v drevnekitaiskoi mysli" [Man in Ancient Chinese Thought]. In *Narody Azii i Afriki* [Peoples of Asia and Africa] 6 (1968): 74–85.

"Otsenki Konfutsii v zapadnoi kitaevedenii" [Evaluations of Confucius in Western Sinology]. In *Istoriografiia i istochnikovedenie istorii stran Azii i Afriki* [Historiography and Sources for the Study of Asian and African Countries]. Leningrad University, 1968, 2: 80–88.

"Dva istoka kitaiskoi politicheskoi mysli" [Two Sources of Chinese Political Thought]. In *Voprosy Istorii* [Problems of History] 3 (March 1967): 70–81.

"Problemy vostochnoi despotii v rabotakh sovetskikh issledovatelei" [The Problem of Oriental Despotism in the Works of Soviet Scholars]. In *Narody Azii i Afriki* [Peoples of Asia and Africa] 4 (1966): 95–104.

"Kak Syma Tsian' izobrazhal period Chun'tsui" [How Ssu-Ma Ch'ien Depicted the Ch'un Ch'iu Period]. In *Narody Azii i Afriki* [Peoples of Asia and Africa] 2 (1966): 76–86.

"Tzu-ch'an and the City-State of Ancient China." In *T'oung Pao* 52 (1965): 8–34.

"On the People's Assembly in Ancient States of Eastern Asia." In *VIIIth International Congress of Anthropological and Ethnological Sciences.* Moscow: Nauka, 1964.

"K voprosu o vremeni vozniknoveniia monetnogo obrashcheniia v drevnem Kitae" [On the Question of When Monetary Exchange Appeared in Ancient China]. In Akademiia nauk SSSR. Institut Narodov Azii. *Kratkie Soobshcheniia* [USSR Academy of Sciences. Institute of the Peoples of Asia. *Brief Reports*] 61 (1963): 96–103.

"Byl li v istorii kitaiskoi literatury etap oratorskogo iskusstva?" [Was There a Stage of Oratorical Art in the History of Chinese Literature?]. In *Narody Azii i Afriki* [Peoples of Asia and Africa] 5 (1962): 133–41.

"Narodnoe sobranie v drevnem Kitae" [The People's Assembly in Ancient China]. In *Vestnik Drevnei Istorii* [The Herald of Ancient History] 4 (1960): 22–40.

"Rabovladenie v drevnem Kitae v VII–V v do n.e." [Slaveholding in Ancient China in the 7th–5th Centuries B.C.] In *Vestnik Drevnei Istorii* [The Herald of Ancient History] 3 (1959): 3–21.

"O datirovke i autentichnosti *Tso Chuan*" [On the Dating and Authenticity of the *Tso Chuan*]. In *Problemy Vostokovedeniia* [Problems of Orientology] 1 (1959).

"Diskussiia o periodizatsii drevnei istorii Kitaia na stranitsakh zhurnala 'Ven'shi'chzhe' " [Discussion Concerning the Periodization of Ancient Chinese History in the Journal *Wen-shih-che*]. In *Vestnik Drevnei Istorii* [The Herald of Ancient History] 4, no. 54 (1955): 116–24.

"K 50—letiiu izucheniia in'skikh nadpisei v Kitae" [50 Years of Studying Yin Inscriptions in China]. In *Vestnik Drevnei Istorii* [The Herald of Ancient History] 2 (1954): 99–102.

"Raskopki grobnitsy, mogil i ostatkov zhilishch epokhi Yin' " [Excavations of Tombs, Graves and Relics of Dwellings in the Yin Period]. In *Vestnik Drevnei Istorii* [The Herald of Ancient History] 1 (1954): 135–49.

"Vosstanie Huang Chao" [The Huang Chao Uprising]. In *Prepodavatel' Istorii v Shkole* [Teachers of History in School] 6 (1953): 57–67.

"Novye arkheologicheskie raskopki v Kitae" [New Archaeological Excavations in China]. In *Vestnik Drevnei Istorii* [The Herald of Ancient History] 2 (1953): 207–11.

"Pokhody Huang Chao" [The Campaigns of Huang Chao]. In *Sbornik statei po istorii stran Dal'nego Vostoka* [Collection of Articles on the History of Far Eastern Countries] 1952, 81–98.

"Arkheologicheskie raskopki v Kitae" [Archaeological Excavations in China]. In *Vestnik Drevnei Istorii* [The Herald of Ancient History] 4, 41 (1952): 152–58.

## Translations

Yin Ta. *Dostizheniia kitaiskoi arkheologii za 4 goda* [The Achievements of Chinese Archaeology in the Past Four Years]. Perevel s kitaiskogo V. A. Rubin [Trans. from Chinese by V. A. Rubin]. In *Kratkie soobshcheniia Instituta istorii material'noi kultury* [Brief Transactions of the Institute for the History of Material Culture], Vypusk 63, 1956, 3–13.

Hsia Nai. "Sovremennaia sostoianie arkheologicheskoi nauki v Kitae" [The Contemporary State of Archaeology in China]. Sok. per. s kit. V. A. Rubin [Abbreviated translation by V. A. Rubin]. In *Vestnik Drevnei Istorii* [The Herald of Ancient History] 4 (1954): 131–42.

# INDEX

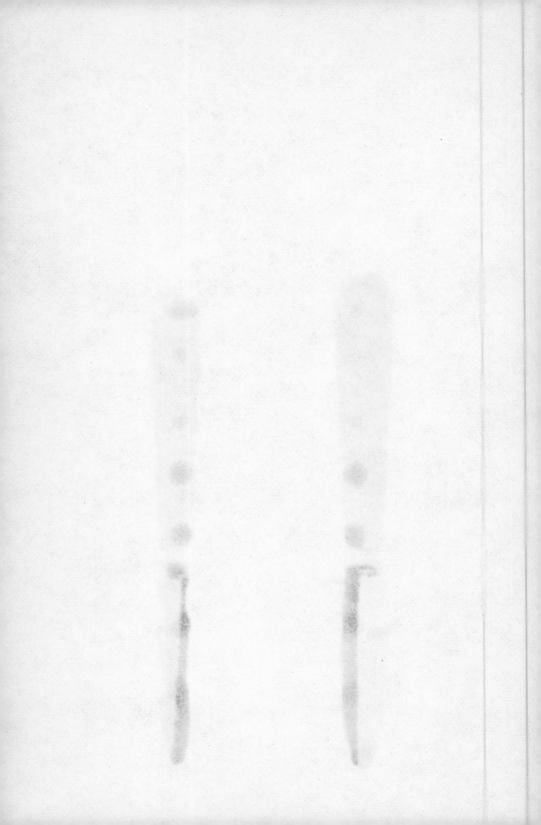

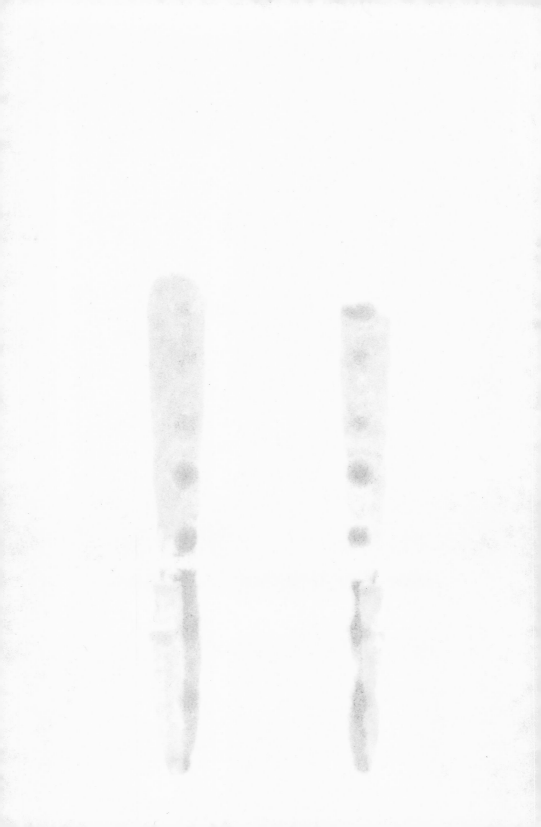

Meeting Wen to Night 16th 6-8 pm
Meeting week to Night 16th 6-8 pm